THE Tropical House

Cutting Edge Design in the Philippines

ELIZABETH V. REYES

photography by
LUCA INVERNIZZI TETTONI

TUTTLE PUBLISHING
Tokyo • Rutland, Vermont • Singapore

Published by Tuttle Publishing, an imprint of Periplus Editions (HK) Ltd., with editorial offices at 364 Innovation Drive, North Clarendon, Vermont 05759 USA and 61 Tai Seng Avenue, #02-12, Singapore 534167.

Text ©2009 Elizabeth V. Reyes
Photographs ©2009 Luca Invernizzi Tettoni

ISBN 978 0 8048 4082 8

Distributed by:
North America, Latin America and Europe
Tuttle Publishing
364 Innovation Drive
North Clarendon, VT 05759-9436 U.S.A.
Tel: 1 (802) 773-8930; Fax: 1 (802) 773-6993
info@tuttlepublishing.com
www.tuttlepublishing.com

Japan
Tuttle Publishing
Yaekari Building, 3rd Floor
5-4-12 Osaki; Shinagawa-ku; Tokyo 141 0032
Tel: (81) 03 5437-0171; Fax: (81) 03 5437-0755
tuttle-sales@gol.com

Asia Pacific
Berkeley Books Pte Ltd
61 Tai Seng Avenue, #02-12, Singapore 534167
Tel: (65) 6280-1330; Fax: (65) 6280 6290
inquiries@periplus.com.sg
www.periplus.com

Printed in Singapore

12 11 10 09   5 4 3 2 1

Front endpaper A pristine afternoon on a sleek terrace by the sea: J Anton Mendoza casts an elegant spell on a patch of secret beach and devotes the far end of the terrace to the Croissant sofa as his "Ode to designer Kenneth Cobonpue". Beachfront Hideaway (page 46).

Back endpaper A clever design surprise in this residence is the ultra spacious upper deck that transforms into a rooftop entertainment area overlooking Makati's skyline. Playful Surprises (page 32).

Page 1 Sophia Zobel Elizalde's dinner setting plays on shells and wine—from a chandelier made with a cascade of *capiz* to the deep burgundy walls ("in the color of wine") to the table accessories comprising coconut shells and seashells. Earthly Delights (page 192).

Page 2 This handsome entryway to a glass and teakwood mansion designed by architect Ed Ledesma is guarded by an assortment of tribal artifacts casting exotic shadows. Exotic Menagerie (Page 24).

Right Paradise translates as a perfectly round dipping pool, a lush garden full of bold and colorful vegetation plus a *cogon* hut ideal for massage! Homeowner Ponce Veridiano calls it Tau Hai Villa— meaning "peaceful" in Visayan. Serene Guest Villa (page 76).

Overleaf An infinity pool seems to merge with the expanse of sea at Punta Fuego. This beach house is superbly located at the road's end and water's edge. Beachfront Hideaway (page 46).

CONTENTS

TROPICAL CONTEMPORARY
THE NEW MODERN

Even though Tropical Contemporary seems like a mouthful of a design theme, it is increasingly prevalent in many house-proud Filipinos' new homes. It's the Philippines' own vibrant color cast on sleek Asia Modern: an eclectic fusion of East and West, a juxtaposition of multi-varied notions, a modern yet organic sensibility engaged behind the fine finishings and new furnishings coming out of the country.

In general, the style manifests itself in a white, modern, open-plan layout, where wide spaces paved in sleek smooth stone or lined with rich-grained hardwood are warmed up and "softened" by comfortable furniture, cultural accessories and personal art accents. When successful, such tropical modern homes mix a mélange of Western forms and designs with an oriental heart and spirit.

Looking for attractive interiors and architecture among the upscale residences of Metro Manila and her satellite towns was an enjoyable task. We went exploring for something new: an Asian or Filipino interpretation of what elite homeowners consider distinctively modern. Instinctively we were scouting for the Philippine version of a tropical contemporary abode, all the while looking out for how the designers themselves interpreted the term "modern". As expected, we found our top modernist architects —Ed Calma, Andy Locsin and Ed Ledesma, Joey Yupangco, Anna Sy, Jorge Yulo—celebrating with innovation. Clearly the market leaders in building Manila's modern new homes are Lor Calma Design Inc, Locsin Architects, Francisco Manosa & Partners and BL+RP Design Architects.

Most of these modern homes are found on the affluent side of Makati, Metro Manila. Often housed in gated villages, those built by the Locsin Architects group, for example, sport sleek

Left Homeowner Rikki Dee's clean, pristine and open *lanai* without walls features an iconic tall-backed sofa by Philippe Starck; adjacent is a modern travertine stone water-wall designed by architect Ed Ledesma. Playful Surprises (Page 32).

lines, pitched roofs with dark slates and a clean, horizontal orientation. They also often sport a subtle Japanese air, reminiscent of the now-familiar Asia Modern look found in Singapore, Thailand and especially Bali, where the style first evolved. Eschewing the indoor-outdoor look of the past, today's versions tend to be glazed with picture-glass windows, but are airy and light with wall-less interiors. Shallow water features cozy up near the house, reflecting their structures in stony pools or koi ponds.

Locsin's stunning Asia Modern style is best seen in the exquisite vacation homes of the Zobels in Calatagan, Batangas (as featured in *25 Tropical Houses in the Philippines*). In this current book we showcase five modern residences built by Locsin senior star-chitect Ed Ledesma and follow through the aesthetic with creative properties from modern architects Jorge Yulo, Noel Saratan, Manny Minana and Royal Pineda.

A second modern stream comprises the work of some neo-modernist or minimalist architects. Generally Western-oriented designers, they espouse a clean modern geometry with strictly linear masses and voids and flat roof decks on top. Modernists in this book are led by Ed Calma, Joey Yupangco, Anna Sy and are followed by some new-generation representatives such as J Anton Mendoza and Gil Cosculluela.

Ed Calma's signature is stamped on Joey and Marissa Concepcion's grand minimalist mansion, an all-white cubist block full of light and space and inward-looking privacy. Of his penchant for vast vertical spaces and minimal interiors, Calma says: "Architecture is the art of making spaces. You should provide not just basic needs, but a dwelling that uplifts the spirit and makes you feel excited." He finishes the classic-modernist Concepcion home with travertine marble and tropical wood, but leaves it sparsely furnished, saying: "The architecture speaks for itself."

Ed is the son of the original modernist architect of the country, Lor Calma. This architect-designer emeritus pioneered modernism in the '50s, long before the style became popular in the Philippines, and his modular forms have grown simpler through the decades. "My architecture is simple and functional," he explains, "Full of light and air. If I have to design something busy for the needs of a project, I will discipline the busy-ness all the more! I like modern, because I like going with the times, like fashion. Modern designs have a permanence. The clean lines of details will last for 100 years and become classics. Over time, my designs have grown less and less—until they become minimalist."

Commenting further on architecture in the country, he notes: "We can compete in terms of design talent, but our technology lags far behind; and we also lack exposure to the world. We cannot do top caliber architecture like a Gehry with our technology. Now we are flooded with new materials and technologies, but still our exposure is way behind the West; similarly, Filipino designers working aboard are too timid to try anything new. Also we are limited because clients in the Philippines are very conservative, so we must always compromise, according to the choices of the clients. Practicing architecture is a constant compromise, never offering full satisfaction."

Nevertheless, despite these harsh criticisms, there are some new and exciting innovations in the country—and some distinctive modern styles are burgeoning *inside* Manila's new residences. With a mini boom of high-rise condos in Makati, Taguig and Ortigas, new opportunities have opened for designers to do their creative thing with model units. There are also some re-designs in some of the many bungalows within the villages that were designed in the 1960s and '70s; in fact, almost 50 percent of the houses in this book are remodels within old sites.

So, what have we learned along the way? We notice that there are multi-varied tropical styles amongst the many homes of affluent Filipinos; there isn't simply one singular trend toward Asia Modern interiors. Instead, we see many diverse directions in the colorful creations of a wide variety of designers and homeowners. Young couples seeking new abodes say they are seeking "modern houses—bright, white and open, but also warm and livable". They want fresh interiors within neutral-toned modern spaces; these are then dressed up with fine woods, high-quality stone and lounging furniture selected more for bodily comfort than visual harmony.

Below Homeowner Ponce Veridiano has a penchant for framing the tropical outdoors from within. One must step out of his villa and cross a stony path to enter the separate "island" powder-room—through a Balinese carved doorway. The washroom is a stylish open-air space fashioned from antique *piedra* sandstone. Garden Paradise (Page 68).

Thus, we term our pluralistic selection Tropical Contemporary—and showcase over 25 Philippine modern homes. We discern the leading lights among interior designers and architects and categorize Manila's favorite home styles into four rough types: Contemporary Chic, Global Eclectics, Tropical Organics and Neo-Modernists—all under a common (pitched or otherwise) roof.

First, we give a nod to the elegant and the chic—Philippine style. Today, ten years into the new millennium, Filipino homeowners still salute classic-elegant standards, as provided by seasoned designers that know their clientele. Total-service designers like Ramon Antonio, Anton R Mendoza and Atelier Almario create a client's abode from the ground up: they create homes that reflect their clients' lifestyles—from the structure to the dressed-up interiors, decorating the space down to the last throw pillow on the sofa or book on the shelf!

Manila's neo-classic master of such looks is architect-designer Ramon Antonio. The ever elegant and sophisticated look of his many residences combines comfort, class and a good dose of old-world luxury. Says the cosmopolitan master: "My style is very personal. I do modern interiors, but they're always warm and livable. They're eclectic with top quality items on display, combining only the latest technology, newest Italian designs and finest Asian antiques. My goal is to *uplift* the lifestyle of my clients, to show them how to maintain and love an elegant home, how to live . . . with quality!"

More pizzazz and less restraint may be found in the residences of eclectic chic designer Anton Rodriguez Mendoza. Popular amongst high-profile businessmen and pop celebrities alike for his über-cool glamorous interiors, his style veers towards "overstatement, ultra-elegance and opulence". A vintage or a glitzy edge isn't uncommon in his work and we showcase two interiors from this luxe designer: his own rebuilt home-showroom in Makati and an eccentric glass mansion on Tagaytay Ridge.

A favorite Philippine style, highly sought after, is what we term Contemporary Chic. According to the social register *Philippine Tatler*, this translates as a home that is "reliably chic and updated, with an edge leading to hotel-like elegance; and sometimes beyond to heightened glamor". Generally urban, this look has been mastered by Atelier Almario, more specifically sisters Ivy and Cynthia who reign as the queens of this fashion-forward movement. With a bit of California-style about them, they are quick, versatile and full of verve. They work on multiple projects at one time; speak varied style languages simultaneously; and strike a warm rapport with clients. They create warm, happy spaces, easy to live in, yet elegant and fun.

The Charles and Ginette Dumancas residence in Bacolod, Negros sports Almario signature flourishes in its dramatic flair and contemporary details. The mansion has spacious *lanais*, water-walls and koi ponds; suite-size bedrooms and movie-star bathrooms; and an illuminated *kamagong* staircase floating up to a lofty mezzanine. Atelier Almario conjured up a breathtaking abode in the tradition of the grand hotels of Asia. A chamfered detail from a tower of the Regency Hotel in Chiang Mai, Thailand was the starting point: this pattern became the inspired genesis of the Dumancas' interior and was duly extended by landscape designer Ponce Veridiano to a trickling water-wall that sets the stage beside a garden of royal palms.

In contrast to such tailored urban chic, there is the natural, the organic and the Philippine traditional —a style that first burgeoned with the contemporary designs of architect Bobby Manosa. His creative heir (and market leader for all things Tropical Modern) is probably the "complete designer" Antonio "Budji" Layug, tropical furniture maker, organic designer, space planner, naturalist and visionary. Layug has long been pulling new homeowners beyond conventional interiors towards a contemporary "pan-Asian moderne" look where a strong love of tropical nature presides.

With his partner, architect Royal Pineda, Layug has led the way with an organic, intuitive approach that works to fully integrate the interiors and exterior of a home. Both say: "First we listen to the land . . . to understand the soul of the site. Then we respond to Nature's given elements, and then honor the landscape with the living house." The team showcases two tropical modern houses here: one of them, the Manolo Agojo house in Ayala Alabang was built in graceful harmony with a giant mango tree, then furnished with tropical chic pieces and choice artworks.

Alongside Layug's stream of "tropical moderne" projects, there's a bevy of designers who are today pushing the boundaries of conventional home styles—toward a look that we categorize as Modern Organic. Beginning in 1999 with the creative consortium called Movement 8, famous for its sleek furniture, furnishings and artworks made from natural materials, the group has gained momentum, all the while gathering new designers with the same sensibility. Furniture designers Milo Naval, Tony Gonzales, Tes Pasola and Maricris Brias from Manila and Kenneth Cobonpue, Louisa Robinson and Ann Pamintuan from points south are all helping to raise the Philippines' design caliber in the eyes of the world. Take Cobonpue for example. He launched the country's first successful "branded" line in 2002 with a selection of innovative furniture pieces that are now seen in many an American celebrity home. His graceful Croissant sofa and kooky Yoda chairs are amongst his best-known works; they're pictured within the pages of this book. Designer Milo Naval is also making bold strides with indigenous weaves wrapped around staunchly modular modern forms. And mention must also be made of Tony Gonzales and Val Padilla: they are making waves with modern pieces for furniture exporters Locsin International and Padua International.

After the Modern Organics come the exceptions to our style categories: designer homes standing alone for their exceptional concepts (one residence looking backward, the other forward). The post-colonial art deco mansion of Anton and Lisa Periquet is one of the whitest but warmest and aesthetically stunning works in our selection. The design of this grand house was the result of an intricate thematic collaboration between architect Ed Ledesma and interior designer Tina Periquet with much creative input from two "very intelligent clients". The house took over three years to build, but eventually realized many visions down to the final details. Tina Periquet, trained in Pratt, USA (and fastidious sister to the homeowner), sunk her teeth deep into this architectural *tour de force* and gave the art-deco house a feel like that of Raffles hotel in Singapore—timeless, elegant and reassuring.

The most forward-looking modernist is conceptualist par excellence Joey Yupangco, a designer who is known for standing in a category of his own. Yupangco generally uses extremely modest materials (wood, glass, concrete) to create minimalist but highly functional frameworks imbued with a thoughtful depth. Primarily following the construction methods of Japanese master architect Tadao Ando, we showcase his modernist space for fashion exporter Sharon Azanza. Azanza calls her new abode a "Japanese-Italian mestizo house", a home that sings a very individualistic song. The designer counters: "Design is not just a performance; the larger part is a cultural communication, highly personal in belief, creatively motivated by vision."

Finally, the most heart-warming discovery of this long book journey has been a delightful return to the warm and inviting Philippine home: that of the tropical contemporary abode of naturalist landscaper Ponce Veridiano. In a new role as architect and interior designer, this top landscape designer has created a splendid indoor-outdoor villa for himself in a lush garden in his hometown of Nagcarlan, Laguna. Each and every piece of furniture in his high stone-walled compound exudes an Asia modern air with the kind of relaxed tropical feel we had been searching for.

Modern aesthetics and the interplay of spaces remind us of his own icons Manosa and Locsin, even while they take inspiration from some of famed regionalist Geoffrey Bawa's design concepts. Ponce orchestrated his landscape simultaneously with the structure of the villa, interweaving pan-Asian motifs both inside and out. The overall result is a harmonious inside-outside living space—nestling majestically in the Laguna landscape.

BACOLOD BEAUTY

Previous pages The grand living room is a harmonious mix of old and new, with the chamfered detail seen in the pattern surrounding the carved door and behind the dining table. The coffee table is constructed from an antique temple door from India while the brass bowls, cleverly inset in wood, are used in Burmese weddings.

Above An immaculate garden-scape designed by Ponce Veridiano of Laguna features 36 towering Royal Palms lining a wide lawn. Combined with giant river boulders and a rounded topiary hedge, they replace an actual fence on the boundary.

Left Landscaper Veridiano so loved Ivy Almario's chamfered wall detail, he extended it to the *lanai* next to the gentrified garden and "floated" a procession of giant carabao jars from China alongside.

Right An upper *lanai* is soigné with rustic casual furniture: Milo Naval's three-piece abaca-woven circular sofa anchored around a wire-art tulip table by Ann Pamintuan. Softly sculpted sandstone cladding on the peripheral walls acts like natural paintings; open to the sunlight from above, their grain is intensely soothing.

"Contemporary Asian Glamorous" is the phrase that springs to mind when describing the style of the Dumancas' home in Bacolod, Negros Occidental. A short flight from Manila, life here is languid and relaxed with a close-knit community that enjoys the finer things in life. Charles and Ginnette Dumancas—business leaders in aggregates and commodities—are part of that community; their new Asian dream house in the south is the perfect base for a gracious lifestyle.

Designed and built by Bacolod's senior architect Antonio W Zayco fusing high quality travertine, sandstone and Philippine hardwoods, the home was formulated on a grand scale. The floor plan embraces spacious *lanais* or verandahs, water-walls and koi ponds; suite-size bedrooms and bathrooms; and an illuminated *kamagong* staircase floating up to a lofty mezzanine. "The clients sought the top quality; they would accept no less than the best materials, regardless of the time and money it took," says the architect.

After the framework was up, Atelier Almario sisters, Ivy and Cynthia Almario, were invited to transform the mansion into a breathtaking residence in the tradition of the grand hotels of Asia. A chamfered detail from a tower of the Regency Hotel in Chiang Mai, Thailand formed the roots of the interior architecture, where the pattern was repeated throughout—it even extended alongside the dining room and *lanai* where it became a trickling water-wall.

No expense was spared on the furniture and fittings: to ensure a suitably grand entrance way, a 6-meter *narra* wood door was set over bubbling koi ponds. This opens into a double-height salon-style living room, the ceiling of which rises to a stepped pyramid at the apex. Further into the house is a gorgeous relaxing *lanai* with views over a pristine lawn and a more formal dining room. The couple are frequent travelers in the region, with Ginnette an avid collector of beautiful things Asian—so ceramics, wood figures, bronze vessels, china and celadon are artfully placed throughout the house, along with locally sourced Philippine artifacts, traditional hardwood furniture and a majestic carved wooden drum from Mindanao. The accents are undeniably Asian, while the atmosphere is international.

The sumptuous back garden, designed by Manila's foremost landscape designer Ponce Veridiano, is defined by a rim of giant boulders and 36 towering Royal Palm trees (*Roystonea* sp), as well as some meticulously pruned topiary shrubs and some smaller palms. Mention must also be made of two strolling peacocks, playing their part in the gracious lifestyle the Dumancas couple enjoy.

Above left A seemingly floating *kamagong* and *narra* staircase with underlit treads rises above a well-stocked koi pond. On left is a towering centerpiece—a majestically carved wooden drum from Marawi in Mindanao.

Above right The dining room sports dark water pools at floor level and an outer "toblerone" wall trickling water. Overhead, a translucent shell band inset with hidden lights offers illumination; it is the work of Tumandok, a craft firm from Cebu. A row of antique celadon jars from China are part of Ginette's collection of fine art treasures.

Left A view inwards from one of the residence's contemporary chic *lanais*. Some of Ginette's collection of Asian artifacts is displayed in a custom-crafted shelving unit, while a light designed from an antique bell sits on a side table.

Right The guest powder room sports a glowing onyx wall and louvered wooden blinds. The amazing sculptural furniture piece is an Italian designer shampoo station!

Far right The glamorous master bathroom resembles a sleek movie star boudoir or a five-star spa. Dazzling white cristone, a reconstituted marble, elegant metal urns and a carved wood panel from Thailand exude contemporary chic.

Above The master bedroom is accented with pierced wood-filigree panels from Thailand, now lit from behind, and furnished with select pieces from Dom Ferrer Furniture in Laguna.

Below left and right Both daughters live in utterly feminine elegance: four-poster beds are dressed with Thai silk canopies from Jim Thompson and walls are sweetly upholstered with hand-embroidered Indian silk.

Above The lower *lanai* features outdoor furniture by Dedon in a neo-weave that is resistant to harsh weather conditions. The dark color is complemented by two fine black lacquered *hsun-ok* from Burma.

Right A view of the rear elevation of the Dumancas' mansion. Beautifully geometric, is rises above the river boulders, topiary hedges, Royal Palms and giant bromeliads of Ponce Veridiano's landscape.

Sleek urbanity has ascended the mountain ridge . . . and now lives, courtesy of a Filipino-Chinese family, in a contemporary glass house in Tagaytay, Cavite. A weekend abode, the home is perched on the edge of a precipitous ravine: Providing a singular experience of Taal lake and volcano, it was designed by architect Ed Ledesma of Locsin Partners. Views are to be had from every point: from the grand living room or *sala*; from the "secret garden", a private terrace built into the slope over the forest; and from bedrooms that sit on the top level of the house.

The new homeowners are a big family who wanted a weekend house to escape the chaos of Manila as well as a place to showcase the artworks and taxidermy animals they'd bought during their African sojourns. As such, Ledesma designed a massive house that comprises a crisp geometry of wood, glass and stone, dressed inside with teakwood or marble flooring, double-height ceilings and picture-perfect views wherever you turn.

The family asked designer Anton R Mendoza to direct them along the decor journey and then embarked on a safari to outfit their palace in the sky. Mendoza joined the shopping forays, guiding them to fill the house with cutting-edge furniture and earthy tribal accents. The entry through a teakwood door floating on glass is a case in point: guarded by assorted tribal figures and a shaggy witch doctor, it exemplifies the ancient African theme crossed with a modern glass menagerie.

Indeed, throughout the whole home, Mendoza mixes modern European furniture with colorful African artworks. Special niches display giant carved masks and statues, while Italian tabletops hold creative displays of ethnic *objets*. The diverse collection is united visually by Mendoza's custom-designed carpet with a tribal motif. The lower-level open living-dining area with floor-to-ceiling windows framing the stunning view of Taal lake is both elegant and eclectic, while the upper bedroom storey is crowned by a massive skylight that illuminates the entire floor.

After a style tour that spans Europe and Africa, one most remembers the stuffed wild animals, who dwell silently in the house during the week. There are stag deer and caribou; a white polar bear; and two white foxes. The animals impart what the homeowner calls an "exotic touch", while the cool, exclusive views provide natural drama.

Previous pages The cliffside residence sports a "secret garden" or terrace built into the ravine and jutting out over the forest. "The exclusive view is what we pay for!" says the homeowner who has furnished the airy deck with indoor-outdoor furniture by Sifas, a French company known for supplying resorts and homes on the Riviera. The olive and dark brown tones work well with the forest backdrop.

Left Sleek urbanity and classic-elegant furnishings along with tribal artifacts frame the exquisite view from the grand *sala* or living room.

Above Descent to the main living level is centered upon a circular Tatlin sofa by Edra in pony hair and a pair of outré Hutton armchairs aside a painting of a Kenyan woman by African artist Chato.

Right and far right Striated white walls showcase a caribou head and African tribal mask as well as modern silver and glass accessories.

Opposite top Cutting-edge furniture from European designers juxtaposes with tribal accents and taxidermy animals. The abstract bird canvas in primary colors is by South African artist Paul du Toit.

Opposite bottom The entry through a huge teakwood door floating on glass is guarded by assorted tribal figures and artifacts. The four small prints are by Federico Alcuaz in mixed media art, *circa* 1960s.

Left A giant polar bear and two silver foxes were especially imported from Yellow Knife, Canada; they are arguably the most exotic of the glass menagerie's inhabitants.

Below In the dining room an Italian tempered glass table from Galotti & Radice is paired with chairs from John Hutton; it sits beneath a steel chandelier from Fontana Arte.

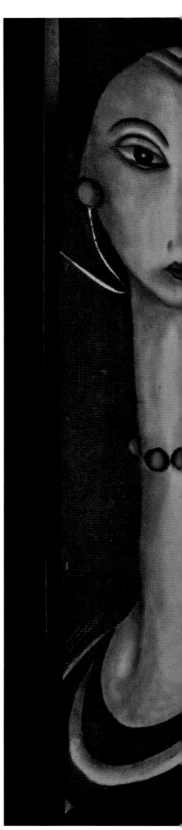

Top left and right An ensuite bathroom contains a tryptich of mirrors and two square sinks. A replica of the Studio 65 Bocca or Red Lips sofa is poised under a Manansala painting of cockfighting.

Above The master bedroom is warm and inviting with natural textures and taste. The wide screen panel above the headboard is a leafy acrylic artwork from Australia.

Above A painting of a fanciful lady, picked up in a street market in Cuba, is poised outside a strictly modern bedroom setting. The silver and ceramic Josephine M hanging lamps are from Metalarte, a long-established lighting firm in Barcelona, Spain.

PLAYFUL SURPRISES

Ed Ledesma of Locsin Partners employs a mix of architectural drama and oriental geomancy in the design of this large home. Building blocks are enjoined by wide water features and cantilevered elements, with *feng shui,* the Chinese art of wind and water, all the while dictating the *parti*. Located in Forbes Park, the house features an angled front gate, a geometric swimming pool that "floats" a *lanai* above its waters and a suspended master bedroom. The *piece de résistance*, however, must be the home's awesome cantilevered staircase that climbs high toward the light at the zenith of this double-height volume—without hand rails. Therein lies the key to the mansion: manifold design surprises that unfold in many corners of this modern residence.

While the interiors were designed by the Locsin firm, the choice of furniture was largely dictated by owner Rikki Dee, a restaurateur with a new passion for design. Dee, a Chinese-Filipino businessman, is eager to mix it up modern. He gathers unique furnishing pieces during his travels, then mixes sleek Italian designs with bright pop-art accents, such as an oversized red PVC lamp by Progetto Oggetto with Gaetano Pesce's Baboon Up 5 armchair. Other stylish finds include Kenneth Cobonpue's Yoda stick-chairs and a pair of Philippe Starck retro wood armchairs. Dee even worked on the design of a golden chandelier composed from five wooden cylinders that hangs in the serene living room.

The formal dining room has black glass panels that slide open to display an ultra modern kitchen with a cantilevered island in *kamagong* and slate, while the powder room sports a 180-degree pivoting door and plays illusively with mirrors, symmetry and automatic faucets. Upstairs, further surprises await: a Japanese-style tea lounge with Tadao Ando-inspired concrete walls and a sensuous massage room attached.

Perhaps the nicest surprise of all, though, is the ultra spacious upper deck that transforms into a rooftop entertainment area. Here, Rikki and wife Beng Dee entertain sumptuously against the backdrop of corporate Makati's skyline.

Previous pages The grand white *sala* sports towering glass sliding doors that open out onto a large blue swimming pool. Design classics here include a pair of black leather Barcelona chairs by Ludwig Mies van der Rohe and an oversized red PVC standing lamp originally designed by Marcel Wanders in 1998 for Cappellini.

Left Another view of the Progetto Oggetto lamp, seen here with Gaetano Pesce's Baboon Up 5 armchair and "footstool". The Up 5 chair is shaped like a large mother's lap, with the stool deliberately reminiscent of a "ball and chain".

Above The clean, pristine and open *lanai* features a high-backed sofa designed by Philippe Starck and boxy poufs as well as two olive green repro Eames Eiffel armchairs. The modern travertine water-wall was designed by architect Ed Ledesma.

Above The dining room enclosed in *kamagong* hardwood and sliding black glass was formulated to specifics from Dee, a restaurateur with a passion for design. Opaque panels of black glass slide away at the push of a button.

Left A Japanese-styled guest house is tucked into the upper level. This modern "tea lounge" features Tadao Ando-inspired concrete walls and large windows with *shoji*-style shades.

Right The ultra modern kitchen was designed by Ed Ledesma: the double-cantilevered island features a solid slate cooking counter (with an infrared range) plus a solid *kamagong* service counter with a beautiful grain. The high-tech kitchen system is by Cuisine Italia.

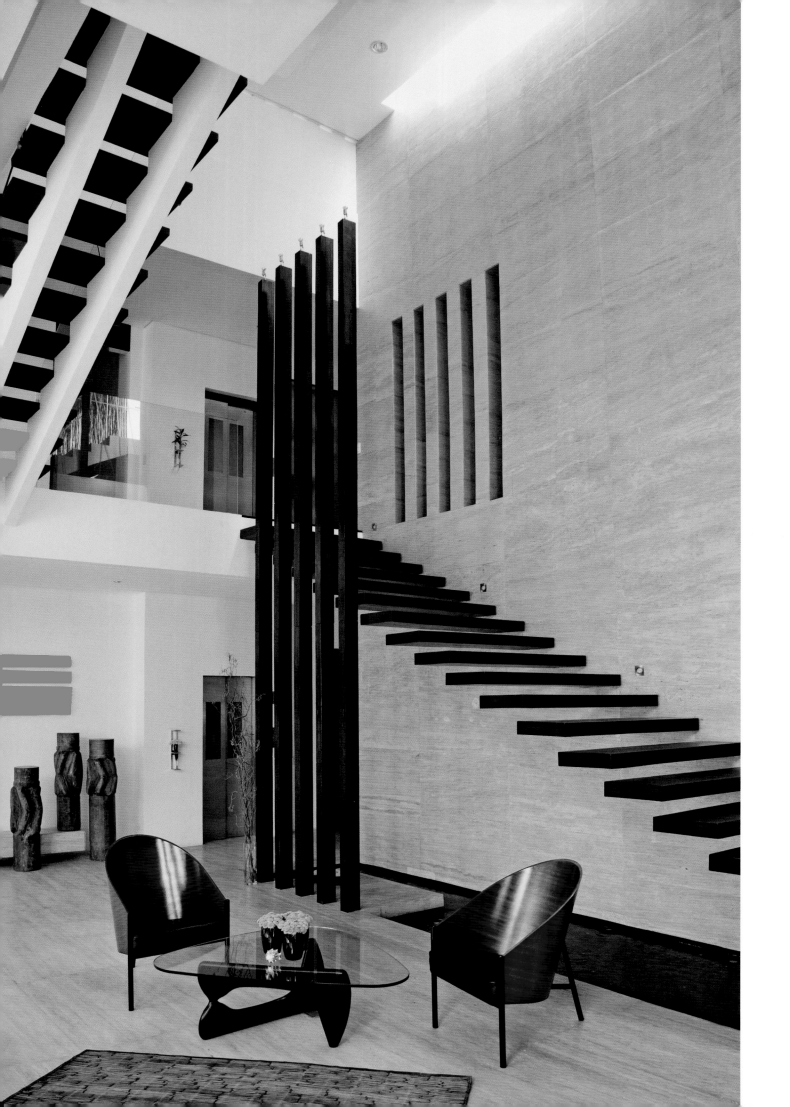

Above The guestroom has a cantilevered bedstead amid more Ando-inspired walls. The room doubles up as a massage room when friends socialize in the outer rooms.

Far left and left Nothing has been left to chance in the design of the beautiful restrooms. The upstairs bathroom is a small, modular space with *molave* planks supporting the sink. Downstairs, the *kamagong*-and mirror powder room has a remarkable pivoting door that opens onto Citterio fixtures and a faucet suspended from the ceiling.

Opposite The cantilevered staircase comprises 21 *narra* treads jutting out from a flat travertine wall and ascends (without hand rails) upwards in the double-height hall. Under the stunning stairs are two retro chairs by Philippe Starck, a black lacquered ash wood and contoured glass table by Isamu Noguchi, and a koi pond.

Designer Kathleen Henares has been captivated by style books such as *Palm Springs '60s* and *Super Potato Design,* so was overjoyed when a friend asked her to create a distinctively '60s-style home for him. He requested she use his collection of ornate furniture, old artworks and Philippine hardwoods and conjure up a retro-modern abode. She rose to the challenge: the house itself is fairly simple, yet the decor harks back to an earlier era.

Located on an elevated corner lot in a suburb of Ortigas, this three-story, L-shaped house has four bedrooms that share a common balcony. The view from the bedrooms stretches out to the hills of Antipolo and Montalban and looks down over a raised swimming pool, a travertine *lanai*, a hardwood deck, and a landscaped garden.

Constructed from stone, glass and steel, the main design feature is the incorporation of salvaged hardwoods in all areas of the house. *Narra* planks rescued from '60s houses clad the exterior of the home and the ceilings of the foyer, while wide *narra* boards comprise the floors of bedrooms, living and dining areas. Thick planks of *yakal* and *narra* double up as railings for the staircase, while further warmth is achieved through pierced wooden screens, dividers and doors. Outside, antique posts form a fence above a rubble wall, creating a textured backdrop for the infinity pool, deck and boulder landscape.

In the interior decoration, creative colors and faux-treatments unify this retro home. The entrance is characterized by huge granite slabs and two massive steel doors treated with a rustic finish that mimics antique wood. The concrete wall of the dining area is faux-painted to match the dark metallic texture of the beams supporting the floor overhead. Bedrooms are decorated with jewel tones and retro lamps.

Furnishing consists of mid-century pieces such as '60s leather furniture, a 1950s dining set, armchairs dating from the 1940s and some ornate bishop's chairs from old churches—all original items that sit well in the contemporary space. The designer muses, "As the client was born in the '60s, when everything was simple and easy-going, the retro look carries nostalgic memories into his new house."

Previous pages A hefty block of acacia wood makes an ultra-solid dining table. The dark concrete wall was faux-finished to match the beams and the black weave chairs. The *narra* wood on the ceiling came from a bowling alley while the sliding doors, also in *narra,* used to be the eaves of an old house.

Opposite In the kitchen, an *acacia* wood table extends off the range counter; it is paired with simple, sturdy matching benches.

Above An ornate 19th century bishop's chair is surrounded by '60s beaten metal artworks, purchased at an artist's garage sale.

Far left Old *narra* tree trunks were sliced down the middle to make a creative screen obscuring the neighbor's view of the *lanai.*

Left Wood casts a warm sheen upstairs with linen and shoe closets with perforated *narra* doors, *narra* Venetian blinds, and solid *narra* planks forming a balustrade.

Above The elder daughter's bedroom has faux-antique golden walls and a rose-tinted leather armchair to lounge in.

Opposite top (left to right) A feeling of nostalgia exudes in a period painting; art-deco milk-glass lamps hanging in a curtained corner; and beaten metal artworks accessorizing the living room wall.

Left A second bedroom has a pink and chocolate theme with daring hues on walls and an art-deco headboard on the bed.

Right The front entrance leads to an open foyer with a '60s Mazzega hanging lamp in Murano glass. Wood-and-glass panels slide away to reveal a space that connects to the front garden wrapped around a raised pool and deck.

BEACHFRONT HIDEAWAY

Previous pages A pristine afternoon on a modern terrace by the sea: J Anton Mendoza's beachfront hideaway features retractable floor-to-ceiling glass doors that open up the interior to the outside and provide natural cross ventilation.

Above and left The designer uses a sophisticated palette of textures and tones in the open-plan ground floor decor mixing designer pieces with personal items. The boxy sofa by Mendoza sits adjacent the thinnest carrara marble coffee table by Citterio. Selective *objets d'art* stand by graphic *objets* of nature.

Right An extra long plank in a grey oak veneer stretches across the room to make a cantilevered dining table—just one example of Mendoza's elegant work for modernist spaces. The slim, high-backed chairs are by Patricia Urquiola, while the brass urn outside is an antique *gadur*, a gift in Muslim dowries.

Designer J Anton Mendoza is known for his elegant modernist spaces that are imbued with discipline, balance and a sense of luxury and glamor. So when he takes that personal discipline and sense of glamor to the raw side of Tali Beach, Nasugbu—to a rough and salty stretch called "Secret Beach"—the results are more than interesting. In fact, his dramatic new digs could be described as pristine and photogenic: With an open-plan living room opening out seamlessly onto an open-air deck with views all around, boundaries between inside and out are blurred.

The Tali beach house is superbly located at the road's end and the water's edge. At a glance, it is a geometric dream: a finely tuned study in linearity, clarity and yes, modernity. Mendoza uses a spare and sophisticated palette of monochrome and chocolate and uses simple cement, tiles, glass and veneered wood with a grey oak finish. Drawing sleek, even severe, lines to define the living space, the modern profile is emphasized by rectangular frames erected against the sky and a triangular swimming pool with an infinity edge facing the Batangas sea (at a rocky distance). All is calm and cool, yet relaxed and and sophisticated too.

Even though the home is undeniably contemporary, Mendoza's taste for classical antiquity—and the contrast it brings to modernist spaces—appears in the larger accents of the beach house. Two sculptural *gadurs* (bronze vessels used as Maranao wedding dowries) are positioned in significant corners of the house; and artwork comes in gilded frames with ornate period sconces alongside. Nonetheless, 21st century panache is achieved in the cantilevered table extending dramatically through the living/dining space and the guest rooms have the feeling of a trendy boutique hotel. The master bedroom takes full advantage of views of the Punta Fuego peninsula across the sea with a long horizontal window at bed level.

As a final modernist message, architect-designer Mendoza presents his personal "Ode to Kenneth Cobonpue": the furniture designer's celebrated organic-modern sofa, the Croissant, sits royally alone on the open terrace—overlooking the dark pool and salty seas under Tali skies.

Above This small guest room is perfectly minimal and minimally perfect. A narrow console table sits before an antique gilded mirror frame and displays an old *sari manok* bone-carving and a sculptural Spanish modern optics desk lamp. The *kamagong* desk chair is by the crafts-master Osmundo.

Left A window on the cove: The master bedroom features a bed from B&B Italia that offers beach views from a low-slung bedside window. Mendoza says, "Trained architects often make better interior designers because they can do the space planning." He has included the outside view in his equation of the room "before the furnishings are added to enhance the structure".

Opposite bottom It's a violet sunset over the V-shaped infinity pool; a time for reflection on nature, harmony and luxury. Mendoza brought his sense of glamor to the raw side of Tali, and now enjoys the awesome sunset from his modernist proscenium home.

Below and below right The evening scene by the poolside is breathtaking, whichever direction you look. The house takes on new dimensions with geometric lines etched against the sky; halogen pin-lights cast reflections in the peaceful pool.

HOMAGE TO
ART DECO

More than any home in this book, this extraordinary example of Asian art deco is a testament to the phrase "design is in the details". From the intricately patterned floors inlaid with marble, ebony and *narra*, to the stained glass panels glowing amber and gold and the ornamental latticework screening air vents and storage niches, every feature is imbued with thought, depth, and the owners' visions of beauty and order. As such, the Periquet residence is an exquisitely handcrafted post-colonial villa in the heart of Forbes Park.

Every facet of the residence was custom-tooled for Lisa Ongpin and Anton Periquet—whose shared heritage and sensibilities led them to commission such an *obra maestro*. They envisioned "a home reminiscent of pre-war Philippine colonial houses in Pasay in the '30s … with the air of a colonial Singapore black-and-white house, with high ceilings and a turreted roof." Architects Andy Locsin and Ed Ledesma of Locsin Partners responded with an elegant urban villa reminiscent of pre-war structures—with soaring ceilings and columned courtyards, fine black railings on open terraces, and the mullioned windows of Asian colonial days.

Tina Periquet, an interior designer and sister of the owner, orchestrated the modern Art-Deco interiors. Inspired by her brother's love for music, she arranged the spaces as movements in a concerto, working out the myriad details until the house sang with musical themes and motifs. Her favorite features are the seven staircases—each with different designs making lilting allusions to musical notes or the frets and strings of guitars and violins. "I have a fascination with stairs—they celebrate passage within the house and make enjoyable the ritual of going up and down."

A favorite space of Lisa, homeowner and curator of the art throughout the house, is the turreted library, lined with bookcases and warmly "carpeted" in traditional Spanish cement tiles. A spiral staircase, with treads simulating a peacock's tail, leads to a loft housing her collection of children's books.

Underlying the motifs and ornament is the structured discipline of a geometry-based system of order—reflective of the character of homeowner Anton Periquet. The detached pool pavilion is his entertainment area: Outfitted with lounge and bar, theater room, guest quarters, and a rehearsal studio below, it is tailored to cater to his love of music.

Previous pages Well-tailored details ornament the spacious living room. White marble floors are book-matched and inlaid with ebony and *narra* wood; fine wood latticework integrates light fixtures and air conditioning vents, and furniture is on a grand scale.

Above The central staircase design was inspired by the form of a church organ. Fitted storage chests are paneled with a stepped square pattern found in the ceilings of the main rooms. This motif is echoed in the coffer-like bar counter designed by Jorge Yulo.

Right The exquisitely appointed dining room is a study in squares with an exotic flavor. The trellised ceiling is highlighted by a silk Fortuny lampshade and the floor is paved in mauve Indian sandstone, bordered with ebony and *narra*.

Above This visually stunning "grand piano" staircase leads to the library. Lit via a circular slab of yellow onyx inlaid into the limestone floor below, it provides a dramatic focal point in the all-white foyer.

Left A pair of ebony *butaka* loungers rest in the exterior colonnade, a scene reminiscent of languid days in colonial Asia. Iron railings and patterned tilework soften the austere white and black setting.

Above left Recessed torch-like lighting, built into columns, creates a solemn, processional effect along a long corridor that leads from front to back of the main house.

Right Lisa 's library is reminiscent of pre-war Philippine colonial houses in old Pasay. Lined with bookcases and floored in traditional Spanish-style cement tiles, it is connected to a turreted loft via an elegant, airy spiral staircase.

Top Wood furniture throughout the house was designed and custom-built by Casa Periquet, the family-owned furniture design atelier.

Above The iron grille work under the spiral staircase depicts the fanned tail of a peacock.

Above Filipino artists' vignette: A Lao Lian Ben abstract hangs at the center, straddled by a pair of carved totems by wood sculptor Claude Tayag. Solomon Saprid's bronze sculpture of a wood nymph rests below a glass tabletop.

Right bottom The gracious villa, with turreted belvedere and imposing courts, colonnades and balconies is reflected in the pool at dusk. Reminiscent of a colonial home, it has expansive grounds.

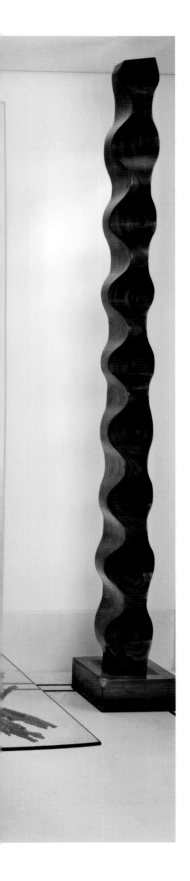

Top left Two square stained glass clerestory windows depicting violins throw rays of amber and gold light into the double-height living room or *sala*. Custom-designed for the house, they were executed by Kraut Glass Inc, a renowned stained glass maker.

Top right The magnificent burl *narra* and ebony cabinet is by master craftsman Osmundo Esguerra. The glass door panel on left came from the historic Casa Vallejo, a Baguio inn long run by the Ongpin family.

Joey Concepcion, CEO and tycoon of RFM Corporation, is a promoter of entrepreneurship and a lover of modernist architecture. He's matched by his wife Marissa who takes care of their domestic affairs, impressing colleagues with lavish food from her sumptuous kitchen. As a team, they live in a giant modernist home in Makati, designed by architect Ed Calma.

Their *avant garde* residence is a massive cubist structure surfaced in planes of travertine, crystal stone and hardwood—a minimalist *tour de force* that reflects the owners' love of living space uncluttered by decorative detail and excess. The grand mansion comprises a sumptuous living room or *sala*, outer *lanai* and resort-like pool area, with a den-lounge and dining room attached alongside. The most remarkable feature of the space is the golden "light-wall" at the entry executed by collaborating designer Tina Periquet. This glowing wall, made of laminated crystal and lit from within, benefits the flow of Chinese *feng shui* energies.

Even though furniture and furnishings are quietly restrained, the house uses extremely high quality materials in the finishing. In addition to the various surface claddings, some have a structural purpose. An example is the geometric treatment of the staircase rising from the *sala*: Calma's "folding walls" of travertine stone merge the floor with the vertical wall and blend artfully into the home's overall cubist design.

Sleek, low-slung furniture, sourced during the Concepcion couple's travels in Italy, continues the grand impact of the minimalist space. Their most unusual finds were the intriguing marine-inspired lamps now floating like abstract white mussels over the living and dining areas. "As we both love diving," reflects Marissa, "These organic forms really reminded us of the sea!"

Owner-entrepreneur Joey Concepcion's favorite part of the home is by the water: on the open-air *lanai* nearby the koi pond with its modern stone water-wall. He loves the sounds of water trickling in the background while he works. Meanwhile Marissa savors her large professional kitchen: with its stainless steel splashbacks and countertops, it is a chef's dream.

Previous pages The family lounge in warm chocolate and gold glows with the light from an onyx bar. The owners chose the B+B Italia furniture for its earthy shades and low-slung comfort.

Opposite The refined living area features "folded walls" of grainy travertine marble—covering the vast floor space, before climbing up the walls and stairs. Note the fine wooden screen on the mezzanine—it ensures privacy, all the while promoting *feng shui*.

Below The homeowners' most unusual find was this intriguing marine-inspired lamp, now floating like an abstract white mussel over the dining table.

Left Marissa's kitchen with its clerestories of light and sleek lines has direct views to the front entranceway. The area is a social gathering place with high stools and counter top, as well as a workstation.

Opposite bottom The understated dining room has dark *kamagong* wood on the floor, a useful long counter and views to a bamboo and trickling water-wall through a large picture window.

Right The master bedroom is an exquisite leather and wood composite of the finest Italian brands—B+B Italia, Minotti and Poltrona Frau.

Below A massive "light wall" made of crystal laminate divides the front entry from the vast, triple-height living room. Designed as a large "spirit wall", it promotes a beneficial *feng shui* flow.

Left The Concepcion's resort-size swimming pool has a modernist "curtain" waterfall, spilling over an architectural lintel.

Right and bottom The spacious open-air terrace by the pool reminds one of an exclusive country club with lush tropical foliage and comfy loungers. It's an area for socializing and relaxing.

Below The well-manicured classic garden-scape was designed by the landscape arm of architectural firm Lor Calma Designs.

GARDEN PARADISE

More than any residence in this pluralistic book, this provincial vacation house is an extraordinary example of Asian Tropical Contemporary—a testament to the Filipinos' varied design styles. Formulated as a holiday home by and for landscape designer Ponce Veridiano, the courtyard home in Nagcarlan, Laguna offers a seamless transition from indoors to outdoors. Blending modern with traditional, practical with romantic and rural with royal, it is a fine example of the melding of modern interiors with lush natural landscape.

An electrical engineer by training (as he could not afford to study architecture), Veridiano came to design via a circuitous route, first selling tropical plants in country fairs. He followed his love for nature and was "discovered" for his special way with plants, eventually becoming one of the country's foremost landscape designers. He cites his inspirations as close to home, Linde Locsin, and further afield, Geoffrey Bawa. Certainly, you can see the influence of both in this project, Veridiano's first foray into the design and construction of tropical architecture.

Modern aesthetics and an interplay of spaces are key to the modest house design. A lengthy approach on foot comprises ascending through a series of stone-terraced courtyards, by gray rocky walls, over white *piedra* stones, and under several bamboo groves. On arrival at the compact home, the entrance is flanked by square columns situated over a two-meter deep pond. Filled with shoals of koi, the pond meanders from the straight edge of the raised floor into the lush, layered landscape beyond. Once inside, spaces are flawlessly stylish, with every decorative item imbued with thought, depth and Veridiano's intuitive vision of tropicality.

The home invites the outdoors in at every turn. The main living area is almost wall-less and each doorway or window frames a gracious garden scene or zen composition in stone, driftwood, pottery or bamboo. Every corner is tailored to display both local artefacts and the outdoors beyond. Hand-weavings, Philippine furniture, brocade fabrics and antique batik mix with Ming pottery, tribal art and modern drawings and paintings—all tastefully displayed in careful arrangements. An interim space outside Veridiano's bedroom comprises comfy sofas and bookshelves in an open-air setting; sheltered by a three-meter awning that collects rain water and spills it into an adjacent pond fully carpeted with *quiapo* water plants, it forms an almost perfect water-garden scenario. As with Bawa, throughout the house what is seen *beyond*, round the corner and in the distance is as important as what is noticed in the immediate vicinity.

Carving and creating the lush imaginative landscape came simultaneously with building the house. Because of its

elevation, Veridiano was able to utilize giant forest ferns, bromeliads and a variety of bamboos as well as plenty of other native ornamentals. Small courts, meandering pathways, trickling water features and pebble-strewn niches are complemented with moss-encrusted urns, statuary and hand-hewn walls. The overall picture is a sensuous interplay between man-made and natural; in the same way, the house relates and interplays with its garden.

Veridiano, himself, has also lived an organic story of creative growth. His first big garden project in the '90s was the Floirendo family's Pearl Farm in Davao, where he was inspired by architect Bobby Mañosa ("the first design icon to awaken my creativity"). Later projects have included collaborations with top architects of the Locsin firm and garden-scapes for the Yulos, the Zobels, the Sorianos, the Cuencas, the *datus* of Sarawak, and more.

Previous pages The tropical modern living area comes without walls and is surrounded by koi ponds and bamboo groves. Pan-Asian materials are seen in the chic organic setting: bamboo is used for the sofa set and ceilings, *piedra* stone for a coffee table, and antique *kamagong* for stools.

Left A hoary river stone staircase—hand-built by Igorot workers from the Cordillera—leads to Veridiano's terraced haven above. The circuitous approach ascends through private courts and lush foliage.

Right The peaceful swimming pool sits amid a vast terrace of *piedra Pinoy* or Ilocos sandstone. The infinity edge spills into the Nagcarlan river, and views are out and over the Laguna's lush primary forests.

Above Every artifact has an Asian cultural history attached. The landscape designer collects traditional bone-inlay furniture, Vietnamese jars, Sarawak textiles, Catholic *santos*, antique batik—all are aesthetically placed in his milieu.

Below left Veridiano merges modern interiors with rambling landscapes. His bedroom has pivot doors that swing wide open over a wraparound koi pond; this is fed by spillover rainwater from the over-extended eaves. Sumptuous Chinese brocade covers the "floating" *kamagong* bed under a herringbone-patterned bamboo ceiling.

Below right An indoor sitting room comprises the finest Asian arts and crafts: Emmanuel Garibay painting in the niche; a basket coffee table by Vidal, topped with a black-lip shell tray by Caronan. Mustard-toned *tinalak* (abaca)-woven covers on a rustic daybed are lit by a standing lamp made from an antique Vietnamese jar.

Above The dining room spells contemporary Asia modern—from the Japanese candelabra and Cobonpue's stringy globe light; to a casual centerpiece of cactus flowers and antique bracelets; to the bird cages atop the exquisite *kamagong* cabinet by Osmundo Esguerra.

Below The guest powder-room is a stylish semi open-air space with rubble outer wall, antique *piedra China* counter, and antique Venetian mirror. A Chinese suamei tree and sexy-pink heliconias accent the space.

Opposite Rustic *piedra* stone pathways meander through the grand bamboo forest, pausing by antique stone sugar grinders that double up as outdoor tables. Ponds, paths and foliage immerse the compact house into the lush Laguna landscape.

Right Veridiano's house within its garden setting—engulfed with bamboo, ferns and giant bromeliads. The designer carved his landscape while building the house, but the lush Laguna garden is taking over.

Below A *cogon*-thatched tea house over the river has its own garden patch of forest ferns and bromeliads—marked with a rustic stone basin with water plants and a stone turtle of longevity.

Above This narrow forest of golden bamboo borders the rustic drive-in parking area—welcoming one before the ascent to the house.

Right Selective vegetation is grown against selective stone walls and very corner comprises a nature painting, every doorway a composition in graphic vegetation. This passageway to the service area is artfully staged with river stones and pole bamboo.

SERENE GUEST VILLA

As his own weekend home in the province became too small to entertain friends hankering to stay overnight, landscape designer Ponce Veridiano designed and built a two-suite guesthouse for his city visitors. Incorporating the same *soigné* ambience as in his own pan-Asian abode, he leveled part of the forested hillside and erected a stylish guesthouse within a separate courtyard and tropical garden. Adjacent the duplex and beside a circular dipping pool is a cute, vernacular *cogon*-thatched hut, perfect for afternoon tea or a private massage. And to entice his stressed-out city guests, he named the abode Tau Hai or Peaceful Villa.

Rectangular in shape, the guest villa has two roomy bedroom suites, each positioned on either side of a high-ceilinged, open-air *lanai*. Views from the front of the *lanai* look out onto a circular pool and graceful gardens, while, at the back, the villa is carved into the hill: there's a roughhewn stone wall, a stony floor, a small pond and giant forest ferns—all designed to natural perfection by the master landscaper.

Embraced by the gardens, guests can enjoy a true Back to Nature experience—indeed, compositions of lush vegetation, mossy boulders and stone walls are stage-managed just outside the two bedrooms' picture-windows. Nonetheless, there's a chic and comfortable modernity about the decor: Tastefully arranged on the open *lanai* are a series of giant earth-toned cushions making two low-level sofas; these straddle a vast, solid plank of *dao* wood that serves variously as a banquet bench or coffee table.

The whole is complemented by Asian artifacts, traditional Philippine furniture, natural woven fabrics and both wood and stone carvings. Antique bird cages house hanging lamps and oversized urns double up as vases with elaborate flower arrangements. Visiting designer-friends just sigh, "Fab-u-lous!" and donate their creations, hopefully to be merged within the exquisite scenario.

Previous pages Paradise translates as a perfectly round dipping pool outside the *lanai*, a lush garden full of bold and colorful vegetation, and a massage pavilion with a *cogon*-thatch roof. You couldn't be further away from the city if you tried!

Right The open-air *lanai* incorporates vernacular materials in its design: The oversized sofas are covered in *tinalak*, an abaca fabric from Davao, the ceiling is of *sasag* (crushed bamboo), and the low-level table is hewn from a giant slab of *dao*, an Asian hardwood.

Below The *cogon*-thatched spa pavilion with its cooling, low shaggy brow sits in a bed of pebbles, adjacent a pair of bamboo daybeds and a series of giant Chinese carabao jars.

Bottom One of the guest bedrooms looks out onto a private mini-garden where stone and mossy statuary and boulders are arranged in artful-natural style. The sofa is covered in Filipino silk and the floor sports a herringbone pattern.

Above The bamboo teahouse by the river is a wholly rustic-elegant space. The multi-tiered *cogon* roof is the handiwork of Manong Carling, an artisan of Batangas; paired with a vintage glass chandelier, it hovers over a simple, but comfortable, space.

Right Another window opening, another show—of tumbling philodendrons, ferns and bamboo by the bedside. The bedroom suite features a back-lit *capiz* shell wall and a funky lamp made from *capiz* designed by Al Caronan.

PASSION FOR WOOD

Michael T Peña garnered widespread attention in 2006 when he won the Metrobank Art and Design Excellence (MADE) Award for Architecture, but he has been a practising architect for 20 years. Built as a family home and erected in collaboration with his interior designer wife Marlene, the home was entitled "The Modern Filipino House" in the competition. Built on a private subdivision facing eastward to the Marikina Valley, the house was designed primarily to accommodate the country's hot and humid climate.

The judges recognized the traditional principles that inspired this updated *bahay* (house) and praised a number of its innovative features. These included a multiplex of large windows accessing the natural light; ventilation devices that keep the home comfortable in the urban air; clerestory windows to bring light and air into the home; wide eaves to provide shade; and vents under the roof to remove odors. An innovative round wooden structure upstairs acts as a giant ventilator, drawing warm air through a slatted cylinder to exit out by the ceiling.

However, it is on the *inside* of this award-winning house that Peña plays out his great passion—for natural wood and all things Filipino-made. It is here that he showcases a plethora of solid wooden blocks collected from islands all around the region; laid bare in their organic glory, they are in-built into the structure and displayed as benches, tabletops, sofas and stairs.

The architect also plays host to a number of local furniture artisans who conjure designs from wood, rope, vines and a mix of other natural materials. Young creatives like Jofel Babaran of Quezon City, Agi Pagkatipunan of San Mateo, and G-Awardee Clayton Tugonon of Cebu are showcased along with modern wire artist Ann Pamintuan of Davao and Rey Contreras, the nature-sculptor of big wooden fish. Renato Vidal, the eco-designer behind a series of outré marine-themed lamps, is also represented. Pena's modern Filipino house is indeed a tropical gallery of organic cachet.

More recently, the architect has added an "entertainment extension" overlooking his impressive bonsai garden. Water features and open-air decks include a gurgling tiled pool for three happy koi and a foot spa for wife Marlene ("There's nothing like a warm foot spa for relaxing and a foot massage for great family bonding!" he quips). As with the rest of the house, it is high-spirited and modern in style; perhaps the term Filipino New Age best describes the atmosphere?

Previous pages Planes of wood with different textures, tones, grains and uses characterize the interior of architect Mike Peña's tropical-modern home.

Opposite A casual dining nook features a collage of decorative wood pieces in the stairwell. A sturdy mixed wood table is paired with modern woven chairs by Jofel Babaran. Further organic status is achieved with a jellyfish hanging lamp by Renato Vidal and fishnet wall hanging by Ugu Bigyan.

Below The entertainment annex includes a warm foot spa with pressurized water jets lit by a crystal stone light-box under the stairs. The whole family enjoys great foot massages for bonding.

Above and right A marvelous interplay of rectangles and rounds is achieved in the Penas' living room where modern art and low-level seating nestles beneath a perfectly formed spiral staircase. The coffee table is made from a block of solid *dao* and, beneath the stairs, sits a round wire Cocoon seat by Ann Pamintuan. The long white mural, with its circular forms, is by the same artist.

Above The dining room is a suite of hardwoods: The recessed ceiling displays Peña's own design, a modular "chandelier" made with veneered *kamagong* wood, while the long table is in acacia. Eclectic chairs are by Jofel Babaran.

Right Peña loves nature and native craftsmanship as evidenced by this light-wall of crystal stone laminate silhouetting a prized bonsai tree. Modern cabinets composed of mixed hardwoods are by craftsman Agui Pagkatipunan of San Mateo.

Above Two arty white rattan chaises with swirling laminated pattern—designed by G-Awardee Clayton Tugonon of Cebu—sit low on the ground by the Peñas' small koi pond.

Right The annex features modern furniture made with natural materials. The earthy grain of an acacia wood coffee table displays two of the architect's prize-winning bonsais. The fishtrap basket lamps are by Vidal and the Sabel painting by Bencab, one of the Philippine's National Artists.

Far right top Another view of the dining room features a large wire accent vase by Pamintuan and abstract painting by Ivan Acuna. The tubeworm glass vases are by a craftsman from Ubud, Bali.

Far right below Peña's modern Filipino house is a gallery of organic design: from this grassy lounging chair with forward-falling tresses, by Renato Vidal, to the overhead rotating fan with pandan leaf blades.

Lor Calma, founder of architectural practice Lor Calma Designs Inc, favors clean lines and organic materials in his work. Initially a furniture maker before branching into architecture, Calma looks back on a career that cherishes nature and the natural world, yet also takes inspiration from thoroughly modern forms. The designer he most admires is architect John Lautner, saying, "He's the best, so organic!". His home, today, reveals influences from the American master.

Spanning decades, Calma's work is still highly sought after in the Philippines. He recalls some of his visionary ideas: incorporating rocks and stones in early furniture designs; hammering concrete walls to texturize them; topping rustic structures with glass. Now, decades later, many of those original ideas can be seen in what he calls his "family condo", a pristine white building that comprises three separate apartments within one structure. He and his painter wife Telly live at the top in an airy, open-plan loft space, while their two daughters have apartments below; all are separated by a shared atrium lobby. And the grand children often come visiting the Calma elders in their arty aerie.

Calma's streamlined apartment is characterized by a fine collection of art along with a treasury of corals, shells and celadons. "All my possessions were made by nature or by man, never by technology," he declares. There's a large black mural relief by Taiwanese artist Chun Ji, his most valuable piece, and a plethora of modern artworks by friends Arturo Luz, Ros Arcilla, Lee Aguinaldo and Federico Alcuaz. The spaces—from the modern, open-plan kitchen to the spacious living room—also feature works from his long and varied career, as do the apartments of his daughters below.

Here, Calma can revisit and enjoy a historical tour of his own furniture pieces: there's a geometric coffee table comprising *narra* and *kamagong* blocks turning in varied directions, a glorious shell-inlay cabinet he designed for export in the '60s, and a quirky horned armchair in *kamagong* and cane-weave. He recalls fondly a giant glass table, the surface of which is etched with banana leaves as it "reminds us of our origins in the province, where we ate our rice served on leaves, with our hands!" The myriad furnishing works are all beautifully preserved—real-life examples of retro art-furniture loved and enjoyed in a modern white condo.

Previous pages The Calmas' lower *sala* celebrates the finest Philippine hardwoods. The adjustable coffee table features solid *kamagong* moving over *narra*, while *kamagong* braces the sofa and also displays a collection of artifacts. Cobonpue's curvaceous Pigalle chaise sits by the foot of a narrow *narra* staircase; the bronze Mother and Child is by Daniel de la Cruz.

Above The architect and his wife Telly enjoy their clean-lined, open-plan kitchenette, where every sundry tool and teapot is an artwork. Two Marcel Breuer chairs face up for modernist coffee.

Right and far right Arturo Luz's Circus painting reigns over a Breuer chair and a white coral from Palawan. The Mondrian-esque black and white artwork is by Calma's architect son, Greg Calma, while the Ros Arcilla bronze sculpture is called *The Rich and the Poor*.

Left It's a walk through Filipino furniture history in the Calmas' condo: A pristine shell-inlay cabinet sits adjacent a Carabao chair, reproduced after a 1930s design by Tullman. Both are early Lor Calma pieces.

Far left The dining room is an ultra minimalist space: A Lor Calma-designed stainless steel halogen light fixture hangs over Mies chairs and a synthetic marble table; while an earthy abstract wood relief by Ifugao sculptor Dayao on the wall celebrates the last supper.

Above A compact mirrored space in restful
monochrome tones displays artworks big and
bold. Left to right: Manunggul jar reproduction;
black mural relief by Chun Ji (a modernist
favorite who's been with Calma for a lifetime);
white marble nude by Spaniard Valdebeso; and
a purple lounge chair and footrest by architect-
designer Warren Platner, a Calma idol.

Left The house entry seen from above, with
climbing vines replacing a magnificent mango
tree that used to embrace the building. The
yellow artpiece is Lor Calma's "Homage to
Calder", the 20th-century sculptor who is
credited with inventing the mobile.

Right The lobby of the family home is a modernist vignette: a giant yellow painting by Raul Lebajo; a giant excavated jar from Batangas; and a bold chair in bamboo and leather weave by Lor Calma, *circa* 1980.

Below A second living room is defined by a giant orange mural by National Artist Jose Joya. Calma's myriad pieces are now classics of retro modern furniture, as this massive table made from onyx laminate from Mexico and the cantilevered console shelf of solid *kamagong* attest.

CONTEMPORARY
CHIC

Previous pages Space and privacy at the rear of the home: Arty big red lips kiss the wooden deck while a streamlined fountain feeds water into the vast swimming pool.

Above East meets West: A modular black sofa from B+B Italia sits comfy between a nostalgic Romulo Galicano portrait on the console and a funky ottoman of lightwood sticks by Kenneth Cobonpue.

Left and right A white acrylic table with rustic wood benches and cane-weave *butakas* is styled by Aida with a chic black-and-white table setting of linen, china, wood and silverware from far and near.

Far left The bathroom mirror takes a new point of view over an old refectory table. Such quirky design turns bring vintage glamor to the interiors.

Fashion entrepreneur Ben Chan traces his Chinese family roots to Pasay City, Manila. He grew up in the family business, earned a design degree abroad, and returned to establish Bench, a highly successful brand in fashion and lifestyle marketing. This model entrepreneur has expanded his market to China and beyond, making Bench the hallmark of a modern Asian generation.

While Bench reaches a wide consumer public, Ben Chan remains a very private person with discriminating taste and traditional family values. So, when he briefed architect Miguel Pastor to design his new abode, he called for two separate pavilions to express his public and private faces.

Chan had employed the same idea in his earlier two-part home in San Lorenzo and wanted to repeat the dualistic scenario. The idea was to accommodate Chan's global tastes with his old Filipino paintings and Chinese family culture—a medley of old and new elements, juxtaposed with eclectic style.

Pastor duly obliged, with a "public pavilion" facing the road and a more private space at the rear of the home. The facade sports a travertine wall under a wide, gently curved roof, while entrance is through a steel-and-glass portico and an antique wooden church door from Bohol. Respecting Chinese *feng shui,* two long deep koi ponds wrap around the house with dark waters constantly flowing. An attendant 150-year-old bronze Buddha statue sits over a peaceful pond, assuring harmony for all who pass.

Facing the spacious garden and retro-modern pool is the back open-air *lanai.* Here, Pastor orchestrates a modern space clad in pink granite with Chan's collections of international and tribal art. Multi-varied fine and folk art *objets* are arrayed on shelves or side tables—and change their exotic displays with the seasons. "It's a very open and versatile interior scheme," notes Pastor. "There's very little actually mounted on the walls (except the mirror and zebra head). It's been designed that way so the artifacts and artworks can be easily rotated from the storage basement."

The myriad mix changes and evolves: antique is paired with modern, ethnic-eccentric with classic-traditional. Displaying his global tastes and Chinese-Filipino sensibility, entrepreneur Ben Chan straddles cultures, styles and generations.

Right A modern staircase sets the stage for a bespoke English Chesterfield sofa custom-decorated and covered by Squint London.

Below Eclectic taste enters the video-screening room: Kitsch Chinese-themed cushions on a Philippe Starck sofa work with a pair of whimsical Tato egg stools by Baleri Italia on a Danish cow-skin rug.

Above right Chan's study is both business-like and homey with a seemingly mile-long conference table—a magnificent furnishing piece where the best fashion ideas are born. A pair of Chinese Fu dogs face two ways; in *feng shui*, such dogs are said to attract success and prosperity.

Right The hallway of traditions: Tall *narra* wood doors, an antique cabinet from Chan's old house, bamboo sprig and print honor the owner's Chinese-Filipino origins.

Far right Eclectic collectibles are arrayed around the fresh open *lanai*: African masks with flower sculpture; chrome chairs with teakwood table. Rotating the artworks and compositions keeps the space dynamic.

Above A relaxing entertainment area poolside spells tropical idyll. Comprising a white tent structure housing a bar, it looks over the tiny blue pool tiles sparkling in the sun.

Below Chan's private studio encased within a towering glass curtain wall comprises a grand library with a spiral staircase leading to mezzanine quarters. As with the rest of the house, new and old furniture and furnishings mix, here giving the room a somewhat retro feel of the '50s.

Above Philippine rustic chic and pink dragon fruit nestle against a backdrop of tree and birds' nest ferns. An old wood *papag* (daybed) is outfitted with chic Chinese-themed throw-pillows from Habitat. On either side are two patrician *butaka*, traditional cane-weave chairs made from dark *kamagong* wood.

Right A gently arched roof and glass-and-steel portico over an old church door comprise Pastor's modern entrance to the abode. A deep pond wraps around the house, connecting the public pavilion to the private.

MULTI-LAYERED SPACES

Viewed from the main road, this Forbes Park house gives a stunning first impression. Layers of dark-tiled roof, reminiscent of Chinese courtyard houses, float above a massive cantilevered portico that thrusts eight meters outwards toward the road. A combination of grand scale, Asian materials and a modern sensibility are hallmarks of this impressive creation by architect Jorge Yulo.

The client, a Chinese-Filipino scion running a family business, is a keen modernist who had the dream of "building a *great* architectural house, as Filipinos did in the '50s and '60s, long before the advent of today's technology". He chose the second-generation modernist, Jorge Yulo, and gave him the brief: "Create a modern Mediterranean house: sleek, white and open, but strong on practicality, convenience and hi-tech efficiency."

Yulo is known as a multi-layered, detail-driven designer. An admirer of Carlo Scarpa, the Italian *maestro* who layers patterns on patterns and uses the multi-stepped form as ornamentation, Yulo's work is no less boldly articulated. In this project, he worked closely with the client to produce something rhythmic and startling; the dynamic interaction between the two lasted almost four years.

Dazzling patterns and multiple layers are combined within a clean modern style, open spaces and contemporary clarity. Even though there are Scarpa-inspired doors and ceilings and a remarkable spiral staircase with tubular brass railings floating over concrete and *kamagong* steps, the home never oversteps its understated boundaries. "From time to time, I toned down Jorge's sensory overload," the client says, "lightened him up when he got intense with organic design and tempered his very challenging ideas. I reminded him of my traditional Chinese roots—I just cannot be that *edgy*!" Many times over, he simplified the decorative details so that his home ended up being the "most minimalist house Jorge Yulo has ever done!".

The beautifully modulated pool and landscaped garden were designed by veteran Frank Borja and the resulting serenity of the outdoors complements the architecture perfectly. And the interiors? Strictly sleek Italian modern with a choice collection of abstract art and sculpture and warmth from plenty of wood.

Previous pages The composition of watery steps, fine oriental bamboo and a textured wall with carefully chipped slates of granite on the ground level was the result of a creative collaboration between architect Jorge Yulo and landscaper Frank Borja.

Opposite The processional approach to this Asian modern house beneath an awesome cubist construction passes through a cut-stone curtain wall and a multi-dimensional wooden door. The artwork directly facing entrants is a modernist work by Eghai Roxas.

Below The double-height living room in neutral tones and warm wood features an overhanging mezzanine floor leading to the bedrooms. The colorful four piece abstract oil is by a young artist named Aris Bagtas.

Above A low-slung sofa set from Furnitalia is enlivened by large expressionist art works by glass-sculptor Ramon Orlina and paper-artist Tes Pasola.

Left The modern minimalist dining room has a geometric patterned ceiling articulated with high-tech lights. The figurative nude on right is by Ronald Ventura; four charcoal sketches of trees hang above an organic arrangement by M Fores. The metal and enamel bowl on the table is from FurnItalia.

Opposite top A pitched ceiling in wood defines the master bedroom, beneath which textured blinds run the length of the room. Modern Italian furniture shares the limelight with outré-bright Klieg lamps.

Left to right The mezzanine is characterized by an art deco air among articulations of concrete, wood and a giant brass art-frame in the hallway. A horizontal window corner without a supporting post lends impact to a rattan-laminate jar by Demex Rattan. The creatively cubist guest washroom has water pouring off a stone plinth into a white ceramic bowl inset in stone.

Above A balcony from the upper ground level juts out over the swimming pool and sits adjacent to the high-ceilinged living room with its floor-to-ceiling curtain-glass wall looking to the garden.

Opposite top A stately and tranquil garden by landscape designer Frank Borja complements the multi-textured spaces of this Asian modernist house.

Right and second right Graceful modern-ethnic vases made of laminated rattan by Demex Rattan make stunning sculptural accents on the ground floor. Intricately constructed with frames of rattan and wood then laminated with natural or colored woven wicker and rattan splits, styles vary from traditional to contemporary.

Third right The brass-railed staircase is a Yulo masterpiece; it is guarded at the foot by a bronze *sari manok* artwork by Mindanao artist Imao.

Far right The stunning tile-roofed portico of the grand house is cantilevered eight meters outward towards the road.

LUXE LIVING

Whilst some opt for modern minimalist, Anton R Mendoza, Manila's eclectic luxe designer, eschews the Spartan for the sumptuous, clean lines for glitzy cutting edge. The Philippines' *Tatler Interiors* annual has termed this return to over-the-top, high-quality luxury as "Global Luxe" or "Vintage Glamor" saying that such interiors veer towards "overstatement tending to ultra-elegant and opulent". Certainly, it isn't something that you could possibly miss!

The designer's home in an upscale Makati village epitomizes this style. After leasing an abandoned '70s house, he took down walls, added a bedroom wing, and clad the entire building in travertine marble. Ceilings soar to maximum height, clerestory windows and curtain-glass walls light up the house, and adjustable dimmers set the (glamorous) moods. An outdoor lounging area features a hot spa near the peripheral wall, and, indoors, the designer orchestrates his abode as an ultra eclectic showplace, collating all and everything new, old—and glam.

Mendoza is a keen proponent of edgy modern furniture, elegant draperies, luxe fabrics, and shiny sexy materials like Lucite, mirror, glass and chrome. These all contributed to the bijou boudoir look he created at fashion store Adora—and work equally well in his own home. Here, he has the additional bonus of a fabulous personal art collection: modern paintings, classic furniture, tabletop *objets*, and antiquity artifacts.

The spacious living room holds four separate seating nooks, each comprising a layered vignette of highly-textured sofas and armchairs (in leather or fur or Lucite); coffee tables with artistic *objets* (in glass, silver, ivory, enamel, metal); plus Filipino modern paintings hung to the ceiling—mainly figurative works by his favorite artist, Bencab. The dining room is no less showy: there's tapestry wallpaper from Germany; a chandelier from Holland; five giant Maranao wooden drums outside the picture window; 14 Russion icons on a taupe wall; and 30-odd pottery jars mounted on Philippe Starck mirrors. The collections are designed to dazzle while you dine.

Asked of his own icons, he names Starck ("who has surpassed boundaries, changed proportions and influenced the world!"); zen-elegant designer Christian Liaigre; and especially, Frenchman Jacques Garcia—"because he's not afraid to be opulent". Certainly, all their influences are seen here, but the overall effect is indubitably personal—the style of Anton R Mendoza!

Previous pages Luxe living with a glamorous edge is epitomized by Anton R Mendoza's living room: East mixes with West, vintage with glitz, sheer elegance with Buddha and Bencab, while glimmering golds and textured layering provide the panache.

Right The dining room features a Dutch "tambourine" chandelier; five Maranao drums outside the picture window; 14 Russian icons, 30 Batangas artifact pots; and a Lucite table ensemble—all elements of "Global Luxe" without doubt.

Above The grandiose living room acts as a repository for Mendoza's fabulous collections: edgy modern furniture, tabletop *objets d'art*, an antique *carrozza* stand (carriage piece) as coffee table—plus Filipino paintings, such as works by National Artist Benedicto Reyes Cabrera or BenCab as he is popularly known, hung to the ceiling.

Opposite top Black-on-black vignette: An outré pair of high-backed seats designed by Boffi (better known for bathrooms and kitchens!) sit enthroned next to an ornamental Coromandel screen and towering abstract painting by Fernando Zobel in monochrome and grey.

Opposite bottom "Vintage Glam" in the ante-room: Luxe lounging furniture, elegant draperies, old and new artifacts, and shiny sexy materials are the hallmarks of Anton R Mendoza's highly individual style.

Above (left to right) If God is to be found in the details, as Mies van der Rohe so famously noted, this home is as close to heaven as you are likely to get: Couples art in paired crystal faces by Baccarat; a matronly Botero sketch complemented by Daum glass vases; Augustus velvet console by Alidad paired with Lalique vase and red vintage Murano vase.

Right An imperial French bed takes pride of place in Mendoza's luxurious boudoir. Ornate brocade wallboard from England frames bedside lamps by Kartell. The designer's pride is the centerpiece painting by Claudio Bravo.

Below Vintage glamor inhabits the Hollywood-style bathroom. Walls and floors are dressed in onyx, the bathtub is in solid black granite, and Dutch chandeliers are in glitz stainless steel to symbolize the tumbleweed in Africa.

ETHNIC FUSION

After Ronnie and Laura Rodrigo inherited a '60s bungalow on a small lot in San Lorenzo, Makati, they sought to transform it to accommodate their new lifestyle—and new baby as well. Architect Ed Ledesma stepped in to update the house: Leaving roof, structural framework and upper floor intact, he dismantled walls, replaced concrete with glass, wood with limestone, and refreshed the old residence with new light, air and modern orientations.

The designer sisters of Atelier Almario then restyled the interiors: The ceiling of the living area was slightly raised, gently pitched and clad with wood-beam details—so it appears higher and "more vernacular". The living room orientation was altered to look outward through a large picture window into a bamboo grove and onward over a spacious paved *lanai* that replaced the previous sunken backyard. At the far corner, the glass slides away to connect both. Today, the Rodrigos entertain outdoors under an ancient *balete* tree hugging the garden corner.

The Rodrigo home is well inhabited by a large "family" of Asian sculptures and antiques—from the outer fence with its heavy Moroccan gate and two Chinese horses to the house exterior that resembles a serene Japanese temple. Entrance is through an intricately carved front door transported from Kerala, India via a smooth driveway guarded by two Mindanao road markers. This also doubles up as an alternative area for spill-over from the TV den.

Inside a cozy character pervades. The home is "peopled" with an impressive array of tribal artifacts from around Asia—wooden ritual figures standing poised in niches or shelves; unusual ethnic items displayed on pedestals or side tables, or mounted in displays or dividers. "My passions are travel and collecting antiques," says Laura Rodrigo, as she annotates the items' provenance. The comfy settings of modern wooden furniture in natural and dark tones support these exotic household denizens. The designers edited and curated the extensive collection, creating stylish vignettes to compliment the chic modern Asian interiors.

Previous pages A tropical garden embraces the house and can be invited into the living room when panels slide aside to reveal only a narrow supporting post at the corner. Thus, a seamless integration of *lanai*, garden and living room is achieved.

Right Looking inward on the Asian interiors: Comfortable seating nooks are complemented by the owners' extensive collection of fine cultural artifacts. The cute floral arrangement in foreground is by designer Cynthia Almario.

Above The view to the stairs: the designer sisters opened up the interior architecture with raffia-shaded glass panels and transparent railings and raised the ceiling with wooden beams to give a warm vernacular effect.

Right Thai silk cushions in olive and gold add a contemporary chic touch to the collection of wooden artifacts. At right, a lucky camel from India.

Above The vestibule with a four-poster day bed features tribal artifacts from around Asia displayed in a variety of niches, shelves, pedestals and dividers. A cow skull from Ubud is mounted on a carved panel from Chiang Mai.

Below left Wooden figures, one a Buddha statue, one a disciple, are displayed on pedestals under the stairs; on left, in the den, under-lit shelves display more exotic artifacts.

Below right The house's two-meter inset from the perimeter wall allows for a scenic pebble passageway lined with bamboo and up-lighters housed at floor level.

Above The large back *lanai*, now paved rather than water-logged, is where the family entertains. A custom-crafted lounger sits beneath the ancient *balete* tree in the corner.

Opposite top left A rustic wooden door from Kerala opens to reveal a seated wooden musician and the other Asian denizens within.

Opposite top right This modernist space with a cane-weave chair and two Mindanao road markers is actually the smooth driveway—which becomes a party area for spillovers from the den.

Right The outer fence is clean, white and modern—and personalized with a heavy Moroccan gate and two Chinese horses. The roofline has a serene Japanese air.

The brief to architect Gil Coscolluela by the young professional owners of this home contained the desire for something "simple, solid, relaxed and congenial ... something different and individualist, but not too far out of the box!". To accomplish this, the architect erected a smart modular structure standing 9.5 meters tall among its older neighbors. Behind a geometric façade colored with two interwoven shades of sandstone, the new house on the block resonates with elevated aspects amid the old Makati village.

"The rectilinear geometry outside links directly with the interior, " says architect Coscolluela. "Inside I used the same modernist treatment on vertical and horizontal elements—so the house feels very integrated and harmonious." It also has a loft-like character, partly because the central living area is double-height and partly because the area is so flexible—it can be expanded by wide doors that pivot aside to form spacious hallways connecting to the next room. Tones of cherrywood veneer dominate, and an intricately designed geometric staircase grounds the house like a solid tree, with its branches of wood, glass and light reaching ever upwards.

Inside, international banker Felix Barrientos and corporate lawyer Reggie Jacinto enjoy a comfortable lifestyle of the modern urban professional, warmly sharing what tennis champ-turned-banker Felix calls their "boutique home". "It's small," he says, "but it contains the choicest items and best qualities from many different sources."

A comfortable, welcoming atmosphere was the owners' top priority. Their giant square dining table accommodates 12 seated in the biggest, widest lounge chairs they could find. "We fell in love with Dedon furniture from Cebu," they confide, and bought it for indoors and outdoors. In fact, the home contains only comfy, lounge-y and kid-proof furniture. "Sometimes things have quirky modern-deco lines," they note, "but it's never kooky!"

The couple opted for a bright red modern kitchen at the heart of the home—and from there, it is a seamless transition into the living quarters and *lanai*, and to non-stop entertaining outdoors.

Previous pages Dynamic space options are a feature of this modern house, as rooms interconnect via hallways and sliding doors. Here, the double-height living room opens into a welcoming dining room.

Opposite A warm cherrywood veneer binds together the entire house, floor to ceiling; tall columns provide ledges and niches for bronze sculptures by Michael Cacnio.

Below A compact staircase grounds the house with its interesting geometric articulation of wood, concrete, metal and glass.

Above The dining room features a square table for entertaining friends and clients who are serenaded by a sultry cellist painting by Vincent de Pio.

Right The compact red-and-white kitchen shines with a cheerful ambience. Sliding glass panels are used to jot down shopping lists and orders.

Opposite top left The *lanai*, furnished with roomy lounging indoor-outdoor chairs from Dedon, is where the owners and friends tend to congregate. By night, the Indian candelabra takes on 50 tea-lights to make a party.

Opposite top right The high-ceilinged master bedroom gets the posh boutique hotel treatment with slick roller blinds and luxurious linens.

Left The couple's office upstairs melds techie and business-like elements with red Chinese accents to bring good luck and prosperity into the home.

TROPICAL ELEGANCE

The elite, elegant style employed by architect-designer Ramon Antonio combines comfort, class and a hefty dose of old-world luxury. At a society party, one guest marveled at his hostess's contemporary chic home arrayed around a lush garden—and sought a similar look for himself: "I wanted color and the tropical resort look; a modern but warm house, not a Zen house," he said.

Thus, the "total designer" Ramon Antonio won yet another client from the Chinese community—and proceeded to arrange his home down to the last detail, even to the last floral accent. Antonio describes his style as "very personal", adding: "I do modern interiors, but they're always warm and livable. They may be eclectic, but they always have top quality items. Nothing has a home-made look. I combine only the latest technology, newest Italian designs, and finest Asian antiques. My goal is to *uplift* the lifestyle of my clients…show them how to maintain and love an elegant home, how to live—with quality!"

His low-profile client embarked on the new project, bringing only his collection of royal history books and DVDs and some Philippine ethnic artifacts. The rest he left to Antonio. The resulting home sports a dramatic modern interior within a lush garden setting on a fan-shaped lot in an old Makati village. Grey travertine floors flow throughout, while a black granite-lined staircase rises to the mezzanine level, where six French doors open onto narrow terraces that wrap around the upper floor. From these vantage points, guests can look down over a white pebbled and landscaped garden, all enclosed within a high outer wall.

The luxe double-height living room is draped in deep aubergine "theater curtains" hanging from the ceiling and features teakwood walls combined with classic Minotti furniture—as designed by Antonio's favorite Dordoni. Ethnic antiques are displayed tastefully throughout the space—Laotian gongs, Thai jars, Mindanao string instruments, and tribal shell necklaces on stands. Modern Filipino artwork is carefully sourced and installed by the *maestro*: a diptych by Lito Carating and abstract sketches by Rock Drilon. The upstairs is no less carefully orchestrated.

The latest Antonio creation—impeccably elegant, yet tropical none-theless—is a welcome addition to this established upscale neighborhood.

Previous pages A semi-covered *lanai* follows the rounded contours of the corner lot's perimeter wall lined with graphic yucca trees and alocasia plants. Modern outdoor furniture by Dedon uses a synthetic weave perfect for the tropical climate.

Left A view from the mezzanine takes in the gleaming composition of grey travertine marble floors, Dordoni-designed furniture and theatrical velvet curtains in deep purple hues. Mindanao gongs, mounted on the wall at left, reference the Philippine context.

Right Antonio favors intimate, enclosed dining rooms: here the modern table set is by Rodolfo Dordoni and the shiny light by Philippe Starck.

Below The sitting room comprises a star-billing of European classical and modernist influences—designer-names such as Rodolfo Dordoni, Roberto Menghi and Le Corbusier. The abstract diptych by artist Lito Carating is installed alongside five Muslim gongs.

Above The formally structured garden is easy to maintain with minimal lawn and only choice plantings. The water feature "floats" two large water jars from China.

Below left The designer presents his client's ethnic artifacts with aplomb, noting: "I like my houses dressy and elegant—even if there's tribal art to be shown."

Below right The front elevation of this new contemporary bungalow is somewhat austere, yet elegant. The wraparound terraces on the second level may be seen above the perimeter wall.

NATURAL HARMONY

Previous pages The tropical chic Alabang living room overlooks and inter-relates with the pool and pavilion outside. It is furnished with Layug furniture—low-slung designs in tropical weaves, polished wood and homespun cottons and linens. The mural painting is by Gus Albor.

Above and right The grand staircase suspended over the reflecting pond rises to a landing and "bends" within a glassed-in stairwell surrounded by tropical greenery. This folded staircase is reflected in a custom-made dining table with its own angled shape.

Left This classic corner includes a Philippe Starck ghost chair; a large grey figurative painting; a custom-crafted glass console table with pewter-finish crosslegged base by Budji Layug; and an iron horse sculpture by Royston Taylor (representing the interior designer as he was born in the Year of the Horse!).

First as furniture maker, then as space planner, the nature-inspired designer Antonio "Budji" Layug always follows his intuition. He conceptualizes space organically (not linearly) based on what nature provides first: "We always start from the *givens*: trees, rocks, landscape, nature's own forms.... Then we continue to the *now*: the moving elements such as air, water and light ... and finally we open up to the *context*, welcome in people and the view, while still respecting privacy." Layug's "total design approach" is exemplified in a distinctive style he calls "Tropical Moderne".

Sharing Layug's fascination for and relationship with the immediate environment is architect Royal Pineda—and the two often work together. Taking into account the lay of the land or angle of local trees, they build and decorate graceful houses in harmony with their immediate surrounds. One recent collaboration is a resort-style bungalow for Manolo and Norma Agojo, business folks who recently moved from provincial Batangas to suburban Alabang, south of Manila. Their sprawling new house affords their family a modern lifestyle that's still closely attuned to the tropical environment.

"The project started with a giant mango tree on the plot," explains architect Pineda. "Nature's given on the lot was this magnificent old tree that deserved to be honored as the centerpiece! We oriented the house around the tree, anchored the composition on the tree … which itself relates to the pool and garden below."

Inside the home, the BL+RP nature-driven design signature begins with the blurring of indoor and outdoor boundaries at the staircase. This is a cantilevered structure that rises over a reflective pool and turns gracefully within a glass-lined corner surrounded by a tall bamboo grove outside. Nearby, an angled dining table was custom-designed to reflect the angled staircase. It's all about harmony, wherever BL+RP can orchestrate it.

A spacious home, there are five bedrooms leading off an upper terrace that nestles in the shade of the mango tree; each continues the organic theme, as does the ground-level *lanai* that works harmoniously with the swimming pool and garden. Here and on the upper terrace, furnishings follow Layug's signature interior scheme: a symphony of modern furniture pieces done in organic natural materials, each complemented by the earthy tones of taupe and beige as well as a plethora of nature-themed artworks and large tropical leaf-and-flower arrangments.

Right and below The Agojos wanted a resort-like abode for the family, so the pool with attendant deck and garden was casually designed with choice lounging furniture. The free-standing hammock—an innovative design by Layug—is finely-woven in polyethylene rattan on a bamboo frame, while a low-slung outdoor lounging chaise with sensuous lines takes advantage of the shade from a spreading mango tree.

Opposite top The master bedroom is a sophisticated composition of subtle greys, beiges and linear black—with a translucent light-panel to the outside and a cow-skin rug as modernist accent. Abstract artwork by Jo Layug-Loignon.

Opposite bottom right A geometric modular sofa arrangement in ivory is offset by the rounded forms of a pair of low coffee tables. The corner lounge benefits from the soft morning light entering through long Roman shades

Opposite bottom left Bathing beauties: A free-standing bath tub sports clean modern lines in the luxurious, spa-like master bathroom. In another bathroom, an out-jutting pristine white counter bears modern his-and-hers shallow sinks with faucets emerging from the oversized wall mirror.

Above Layug's organic-classic Cluster Bamboo table acts as host to some textured tropical Carlotta Host chairs.

Right This dark, bulbous pod of a woven sofa and side table on an outer deck were purchased in Cebu by the Agojo family.

LIGHT AND WATER

This modern white bungalow in Corinthian Hills, north of Manila, combines interesting concepts of space, light, water—and tropical nature. From the start, designer Budji Layug and architect Royal Pineda were challenged to build a *modern* home within a "Mediterranean" profile—the designated style of the village! Despite tight building restrictions, the BL+RP team squeezed *five* split levels of living space fused together within modern blocks under a typical tiled roof—and surrounded them with an open garden ambience.

Water and bamboo play vital roles in this modern, virtually transparent house owned by Mr and Mrs Joaquin Yap. From the front gate, one views the massive volume of the glass-curtained living room that seems to "float" on gurgling waters that wrap around the home. Pool waters trickle off one edge making for a refreshing fountain, while big clerestory windows—massive triangles open to the sky—bathe the house in natural sunlight that filters through the bamboo grove.

Inside, the living room reposes stylishly under an atrium ceiling—a contemporary setting surrounded by "bamboo walls". Pineda explains the effect as "like living in a tropical garden within the city". This effect is furthered by an outdoor pool extending a channel indoors and thereby defining a foyer area. In the same room, on a wall that screens the stairwell is a giant mural painting by Layug—a massive hourglass image, rich and sensual with flowing textures and golden-orange tones.

"It's actually a compact house designed with five intervening and interspersed levels," says Pineda, "but as there's much visual connection throughout, the space feels warm and intimate for the family." He is most proud of the staircase that weaves in and out of view between levels, giving "both privacy and mystery". "Yet it's light and friendly," he notes, "climbing within the bamboo."

The Yap home was one of the first collaborations of the new design-tandem of BL+RP. It combines Pineda's modernist concepts from the days when he worked in the Locsin firm with Layug's tropical organic style that is his global trademark. Since meeting six years ago, architect and designer have blended their abundant talents seamlessly. Here, they meshed their natural organic sensibilities and flowed creatively—much like the sensuous hourglass on Joaquin Yap's wall.

Previous pages The Yap's see-through living room as viewed from above. A tranquil room, it appears almost like a platform "floating" on water. Textures include leather, cow-hide, soft cotton, woven organics, stone and water.

Right The simple, rectangular dining room features a wooden table with a transparent glass center surrounded by chairs with woven backs from the Budji collection. The painting on the left is by the homeowner.

Top, above middle and above Layug and Pineda brought modern hotel-like details into the Yap home as exemplified by the long tight staircase that's hidden from view, the guest washroom with a modernist sloping sink and laminate crafts from modernist designers using natural materials.

Left top and bottom The house structure compacts *five* interspersed floors under a Mediterranean-style tiled roof. One can peek into multiple all-white levels at one time—and gaze on giant paintings or sculptures marking the next floor.

Opposite Modern craftsmanship in natural indigenous materials: The assorted wire tree sculptures by Ann Pamintuan stand aside a modular table and bench setting designed by Milo Naval.

VERNACULAR NOSTALGIA

When long-term expatriate Filipinos, Danilo and Mellissa Gervacio, decided they wanted to build a modern home at home (as it were) they were keen to incorporate some of the "old Filipino traditions they had left long ago." Noel Saratan was the architect of choice. Known for his Asian-inspired architecture, this was Saratan's first project on a small urban plot. He rose to the challenge with the design of a modern white bungalow under four pitched roofs in dark slate and a nostalgic vernacular-oriented interior.

While the home's exterior profile spells a crisp clean linearity in concrete and glass, the inside story is warm, rustic and textured—with wood and grass weaves, *capiz* shell and red terracotta tiles. This look is furthered by organic-modern furniture and artefacts sourced from designer and artist friends based in Manila and Cebu; these include Tony Gonzales, Louisa Robinson, Maricris Brias, Impy Pilapil, Jeannie Goulbourn, Karlo de los Reyes, Vincent Padua and Eric Paras, but most specifically Milo Naval. The creative paper-artist Tes Pasola, a member of the illustrious Movement 8 design consortium that helped promote Filipino designs globally, was given the task of co-ordinating the sourcing.

The core of the home is an open-plan, airy *sala* or living area. It sports a soaring double-height pyramidal ceiling fully lined with all-natural *arurog* poles derived from *cogon* grass and floors of traditional red Vigan tiles. Several large wood lattice panels serve as accents and to conceal air-conditioning units; they remind the Stateside owners of the old-fashioned *capiz* windows found in the Philippines' *provincia*. In this room, the textured look is furthered by the choice of furniture, in this case Naval's Luce set—a low-lying sofa set wrapped in woven *t'nalak*, a modernized ethnic abaca fabric from Davao.

All other areas of the home take their design ethos from this central core: In the adjacent *lanai* Naval's majestic modern dining table comprises a massive block of *dau* wood standing freeform on stainless steel-clad stands; paired with dark *tinalak*-covered dining chairs, it epitomizes Naval's desire to mix the technological with organic materials. Elsewhere, modern is fused with rustic in furnishings utilizing native materials—tropical woods, paper, vines and shells—as well as the innate all-Filipino design ingenuity. This is further exploited in the choice of artefacts: Everywhere you look, the Philippines is celebrated in myriad ways.

Previous pages A colorful symphony of Filipino organic designers converges in the living room finished with vernacular touches of wood, *capiz* shell and Vigan tiles. A modern touch is achieved by the steel and black glass tables designed by Milo Naval of OMO; he is also responsible for the sofa set in *tinalak* weave.

Left Rooms are outfitted with all-natural, hand-woven fabrics—from Milo Naval's sofa upholstered in a paper and *sinamay* fabric from Bicol to the gossamer Philippine silk fabrics used as drapes from Jeannie Goulbourn of Silk Cocoon Manila.

Right Beneath a panelled window sits a winged Ruben chaise finished with natural abaca fiber, while the cone-based Roberti coffee table is woven from a polypropylene resin known as viro. Both from Padua International. The shaggy rug comes from Natuzzi at MOS Design.

Below Feeling at home on the red Vigan-tiled flooring: Industria work table and rustic stool with metal accessories by Eric Paras of A11.

Left A bathroom setting includes counter and console in Philippine mahogany. There's a bamboo-lined outdoor shower beyond the glass door and *buho* grass poles lining the ceilings (these can be seen in the angled side mirror).

Below Triboa bedroom set in neutrals features a wraparound headboard resembling a rattan screen. Two bulbous steel side tables with white ash tabletops carry modernist black-stone ball lamps by Leo Almeria. All from the Triboa Bay Living line by Eric Paras.

Above (left to right) Accents in the Gervacio home read like a *Who's Who* of the Filipino and international design worlds: Brass leaf and plate accents with mother-of-pearl shards by Tony Gonzales; table lamp made from textured off-white paper from Vitra at MOS Designs; mother-of-pearl jewelry centerpiece by Hans Brumann; and snakeskin accessory boxes by Louisa Robinson.

Below Minimalist wood furniture from Triboa Bay: work table of solid white ash wood and solid steel legs, with leather-woven square chair by Eric Paras. Modernist paper artworks here, in bedroom and *sala* are by Tony Gonzales.

Opposite top The garden is ever present in the home, as seen here from the *lanai*. The giant banquet dining table made from *dao* hardwood upon stainless-clad stands, the black *tinalak*-upholstered dining chairs, and printed leather-weave bench (unseen) are by designer Milo Naval.

Opposite bottom far left and left Giant cylindrical planters by Carlo de los Reyes of Ezra give the room a rustic modern character, while the natural world is echoed in a collection of leafy decorative cushions in *tinalak* weave with coconut beadwork; by Maricris Brias of Tadeco.

Opposite bottom right Low-slung red accent chair in textured *tinalak* by Milo Naval; the antique wooden filing cabinet behind is from A11.

Below An extraordinary ethereal light in origami paper, designed by Louisa Robinson, resembles the outline of a dragon. It illuminates a black basket seat by Tony Gonzales for Locsin International.

ANDO-INSPIRED ABODE

Valle Verde comprises several residential villages near Ortigas Center, the business hub of the northeastern metropolis. It offers a variety of plots on gentle slopes that allow one to experiment with space, place and time. In this modern structure, architect Joey Yupangco has pushed the limits of his architectural ideas to create a living, breathing house "with a global perspective". Inspired by the construction methods of the Japanese master architect Tadao Ando, he uses just three modest materials—glass, cement and wood. The resulting spaces are flexible and functional—and zen-like in their relaxed simplicity.

Essentially, the two-story residence of Sharon and Fritz Azanza is a giant glass box, fully clad with curtain-glass walls wrapped around a core of functional rooms. In spite of its strictly modernist ethos, the house reflects a dynamic interface between nature and the home. "I'm trying to reconcile modernism with the tropical conditions in this country," says Yupangco. "But I've come to realize I'm a situationist too, as every condition differs. Architecture is not just about the building, but all else within and around of it also." Reflecting his thoughts, the home is designed with an outer border of wide corridors that allows those indoors to walk near a bamboo grove outdoors—separated only by sheet glass. "It's like walking amid the trees!" says Yupangco.

The inner walls wear an ash-gray concrete finish throughout—the result of using Ando's cast-in-place process—while transparency is shielded by the installation of a double-layer sunscreen device. This ensures privacy and also casts varying patterns of light and shade on different surfaces in the home. The louvers also bring warmth into an otherwise austere structure. In keeping with the Japanese ethos, the home keeps surface ornamentation minimal and there are plenty of hidden storage spaces in many of the rooms.

For the interiors, Yupangco interfaced well with the creative eye of homeowner Sharon Azanza, an art-collector and businesswoman who exports Made-in-Philippines fashion handbags to the world. She delighted in co-planning this radical new space and stoked up her own modernist instincts to furnish the family house with selective collections. Many of the whimsical Italian furniture pieces came from the House of Driade in Milan, where she drops by after attending the annual Milan trade shows.

Azanzo describes herself as being "inspired and guided by Joey", but has clearly left her own individual stamp on the home. "The house is a real mixture, a Japanese and Italian *mestizo*," she says, but it is better called "global". The furniture is mainly modern Italian, surfaces are generally plain, and the outside bamboo is a constant inside. As such, it's a good example of how creative collaboration between architect and owner can garner unusual results.

Previous pages The restful living room offsets austerity with luxury, the hard with the soft. A pair of pristine, cotton covered Sweet Nothing sofas designed by Philippe Starck for Driade hug a low glass coffee table displaying a selection of glassware, the work of Borek Sipek.

Above Connected to a small deck and large lawn, the living room constantly invites the outside in—there's transparency, tropicality and modern, easy living here.

Left Inspired by Ando's cast-in situ methodology, designer Joey Yupangco built the two-story house as a giant light box, employing a sunshade effect on the vertical glass windows to cast geometric shadows into the interior.

Right The cast in-situ wall blocks work to zen effect with a front door of solid Philippine mahogany. The three artworks at the left of the entrance are by Lao Lian Ben, a Filipino-Chinese artist.

Above Every room, including the wonderfully clean-lined, spacious kitchen is space-planned for functionality. With masses of storage and a modern counter-top with hob and sink, the room is a hub for socializing while cooking. The four ultralight sled-base chairs are from the Juliette range designed by Hannes Wettstein for Baleri.

Left The modern dining room with arresting chandelier sports a number of hidden storage devices. Vertical panels of translucent glass on left conceal a cabinet for cutlery and china, while the stepped translucent glass panels on right articulate the second stairway behind the concrete wall; the inside niche is also used for storage.

Right The family room gravitates around a mustard sofa and spring-inspired carpet by Locatelli. A staircase goes light-footed towards the bedrooms, while a double-lined window shade system plays with light seeping through the glass.

Right The baroque-style powder room with Viennese mirror, royal trimmings and chrome fittings is an ornate breakaway from the minimalism found in the rest of the house.

Below A modern-oriental feel in the master bedroom is achieved with a padded wallboard made from Japanese silk brocade installed over a wide bed "afloat" on acrylic legs.

Far right A corner in the den features a Faust stool by Mario Bellini for Driade; the tea set in foreground is by Zani & Zani.

Right below A geometric cantilevered staircase leads up to the second story. With a slim handrail and views to the bamboo grove, it gives a "floating", light effect.

Above At night, the structure appears like an open-sided doll's house built in glass. Transparency is omnipresent: the master bedroom on the upper right has a vantage point over the rest of the the entire house, including the kitchen at lower left.

Below left Clean, minimal and austere, this bathroom is dressed in pristine concrete and white ceramic.

Below middle A long tall staircase ascends by the curtain-glass wall that wraps around the rear of the house. The windows and sunscreen devices create varying patterns of light throughout the day.

Below right Tropical fruit and flowers and colorful Italian furniture bring vibrancy to the cool gray *lanai*.

TIMBER HAVEN

When a young CEO who harbors a love for scuba diving, the great outdoors and fine Philippine hardwoods decided to go it alone in designing and building a new home, he had more than his fair share of misgivings. Describing himself as "a frustrated architect", the plan was not without its risks. Happily, the result is to his liking. "My wife and I are both divers and love the beach. We wanted to recreate the feeling of being in a resort, in a home that's wide open to nature and the outdoors, with a relaxed feeling all around."

First of all, the intrepid owner had to dismantle an existing Spanish-style house, but sensibly he retained the footprint and rebuilt the house along the same plan with the creative gumption of a do-it-yourselfer. "It was all *mano-mano* (hands-on) designing", he says. "No contractor, no paperwork, no plans. We simply took things down if they didn't work and tried something different." Luckily, he had access to some professional advisors—architect Ed Ledesma and landscape designer Ponce Veridiano—so the program wasn't without expertise.

The end result is a free-flowing home with minimal divisions. Walls have been replaced with large sliding panel dividers in a variety of timbers and French windows connect the interiors with the garden. The vast teakwood floors were the biggest investment in the house and give the home warmth and character. "We had to bite the bullet to proceed with our dream of golden teak," says the owner. Other wooden treasures include blocks of Philippine hardwood collected over the years, ironwood benches, solid *dau* for the dining table, and *kamagong* for the sideboards.

A stunning feature in the interior is the grand architectural staircase. Five-meter wide steps climb to a five-meter wide landing, before turning up into the bedrooms. Elsewhere, exotic Asian details merge into the modern framework: an intricate Javanese doorframe doubles up as the entry portal from the driveway and Burmese "rose windows" become carved wooden accents in open-air shower rooms. Even the kitchen employs a creative adaptation inspired by the cockfighting arena: its wooden ceiling with tiny slats encourages ventilation in and out of the roof.

Bright, airy and inviting, the home is a repository of "ideas picked up from my travels" explains the owner. As such, it is an ideal base for his growing family—and an interesting architectural statement to boot.

Previous pages The warmth of wood permeates throughout the teakwood music room. A pair of Ilocos armchairs and a simple glass table comprise the furnishings, allowing the modernist waterfall beyond the glass to take center stage.

Left The grand minimalist staircase in wall-to-wall teakwood is one of the home's more interesting features. On right a forest painting by Steve Soler complements a bronze figurine on an ironwood bench.

Above The owner's art collection in the sitting room features works by his favorite artists, Joy Mallari and Marcel Antonio.

Right A whimsical wire flower stand by Kenneth Cobonpue lines a wall in the spacious hallway.

Far right A laminated *capiz* tea set in pop-art hues signals the couple's taste for bright modern accents. Behind are a pair of chunky Philippe Starck Bubble Club outdoor armchairs.

Below Modernist painter Ivan Acuna's 6' x 14' mural in orange and gold complements the giant 12-seater dining table in *dao* hardwood.

Bottom A clean-lined minimalist kitchen with floating bar for preparation, plating and presentation is a chef's dream. Melamine tops and splashbacks are both practical and aesthetic.

Above The family's TV lounge with a fuschia settee set extends onto a wooden deck, enlivened with more modern pop-art colors. The Bubble Club chairs recall classic Chesterfield styling in colorful, weatherproof, UV-resistant polypropylene and are manufactured in Italy by Kartell. The deep teak bench sports complementary colored covers.

Right Wooden slatted screens and "privacy walls" with pierced panels block the views between balconies and rooms upstairs.

EAST-WEST BLEND

Previous pages Kenneth Cobonque's sinuous Croissant sofa and abaca-twine seat are paired up with Milo Naval's cushioned bench with sliding tabletop in the living room. Ann Pamintuan's wire-art pieces on the cantilevered console sit before a nascent bamboo grove.

Above Cream, ivory and beige form a neutral color scheme for this part of the living room. Natural cow-hide ottoman and cushions by Natuzzi complement the *Open Landscape from Satellite* mixed media work by Ruel Caasi.

Left Naval's four-poster daybed wrapped in Davao abaca weave sits before a low wrought-iron table by Trek Valdizno. On right is a bold red painting by the master Ang Kiukok.

Right The designers updated the family's heirloom table by remounting the top on a shiny modern stand. The cheerful fruit and food paintings—appropriate fodder for a dining room—are by Ang Kiukok.

When it came time to renovate their sprawling but traditional home in Ortigas, Mr and Mrs Tan called on Ivy and Cynthia Almario to update and redesign the interiors. In the past the Almarios had successfully collaborated on several projects for the Tan couple's different business ventures; now they were charged to rework the house for a "zestful" new lifestyle.

For structural renovations, architect Ed Ledesma was brought on board to transform the cluttered family home into something altogether more sleek and sophisticated. An instant facelift was achieved through the installation of stately white marble floors, and improvements to the facade further helped. Here, the outer fence was covered with horizontal bands of travertine stone and large wooden doors installed so that they seem to "float" at the glass-fronted façade. Favorable *feng shui* flows were thereby encouraged.

Further adjustment continued within, and today there's a refreshing openness to the East-meets-West designer spaces. The entrance is anchored by a contemporary abstract in white, backed on the reverse by a giant wire "moon" by Ann Pamintuan. From here it is a seamless transition into the spacious *sala* or living room that gives over into a wide *lanai*, connected to both the dining room and the big back garden. Rooms flow from one to the other, without divisions, and a set of *narra*-framed sliding glass doors with structural posts clad in golden wood separate the *lanai* from the garden.

The Almario sisters have styled the free-flowing spaces with a veritable gallery of tropical modern Philippine furniture. The *sala* comprises three separate settings forming a style progression toward large picture windows with views of an exterior bamboo grove. In the first section, a luxurious white sofa by Natuzzi is accented with cow-skin furnishings and modern artwork. This is followed by the natural *tinalak*-weave Banig sofa by Milo Naval, and finally, the organic-modern Croissant sofa by Kenneth Cobonpue.

On the wide *lanai*, a lime-green table setting from the Yoda collection by Cobonpue looks out over the pool and garden landscaped by Ponce Veridiano. On the opposite side, a picture-glass alcove shelters a white porcelain statue of the Chinese goddess Kuan Yin, sitting three feet high on a black enamel console. For homeowners Mr and Mrs Tan, she preserves peace and harmony in their modern new home—all the while anchoring the family to their roots.

Above The softly tailored chocolate-toned guest bedroom is illuminated by spots and anglepoise lights, as well as indirect lighting behind its floating ceiling and shelves.

Opposite top The iconic high-backed Yoda stick chairs by Cobonpue accent many modern homes. Note the seamless flow of space around architect Ledesma's wood-clad columns into the lush garden designed by landscape designer Ponce Veridiano.

Right Davao artisan Ann Pamintuan crafted the giant wire-art "moon" rising over a luscious white leather armchair by Natuzzi.

Second right The circular forms of several abstract artworks are to be seen at the spirit wall by the front entry; they signify a welcome to the Tan family's free flowing home.

Third right and far right Zestful floral arrangements by designer Cynthia Almario are presented with modern accessories of glass, chrome and acrylic. Small fruit paintings are by homeowners' favorite artist, Ang Kiukok.

GRAPHIC DESIGN

Tasked with creating a type of "Vintage Glamor design" on a shoestring budget, architect-designer Joy P Dominguez dug deep into her imagination for creativity—and results. She shopped around, economized, was inventive and resourceful. She transformed the ordinary with strong colors; took risks with bold patterns and outré combinations. These are the high-spirited methods Dominquez used to decorate a high-rise condo—now waiting for the right tenant.

"I started with a French-stylized acrylic black chandelier I bought in Singapore," explains the constant shopper. "Then I sought to match it with bold graphics on the *sala* wall and sofa." She looked around long and hard to source the right black-and-white striped material, had it upholstered on the sofa, then commissioned surface-artist Genalyn Bocar to hand-stencil one long wall. Choosing a black graphic pattern reminiscent of a Chinese coin, she proceeded to accessorize with further black-and-white accents: a calm wooden Buddha under an oriental-style lampshade, a black urn on a white column, a white-and-steel Wassily chair (still looking modern today, although the original was designed in 1925 by Marcel Breuer!). The juxtaposition works, the glamor succeeds.

Dominguez is never the minimalist, but rather a bright-eyed colorist who revels in giving paint free rein in her interiors. Her bias for strong, colorful tones shows up in the bedrooms—the master bedroom is painted with a lime green trellis on the wall, the children's bedroom is dominated by a hand-stamped Chinese decorative motif.

"Saving money drives creativity," the designer muses. "But what you *most* need to spend is *time*." Luckily, Dominguez is an avid browser, ever on the prowl for decorative items and glamor accents. Even when there's no project on, she's out doing the rounds, scouring shops for overruns and remainders with distinctive character. When she came upon Kerry Whistler's book *The Art of Unexpected Style,* she felt vindicated for her methods and styles. "Designing with the spirit of surprise is my style!" she realized.

Previous pages Chinese coin graphics and bold modern stripes dominate in a living room that mixes modern pieces with a few Asian classics (local baskets, Chinese wedding cabinet) and just a touch of Chinoiserie chic.

Left East and west merge in this spiffy black-and-white themed living room, vibrantly decorated high up in Fort Bonifacio.

Right The bedroom gets a garden trellis wall in lime green, as painted by surface artist Genalyn Bocar. The old Chinese armoire is the only true antique in the condo.

Below The condo's lounge is a study in warm browns with accents of red lacquered Orientalia. The low Ming-style coffee table works well with the Arturo Luz abstract.

ART HAVEN

Ayala Alabang is a residential development located about 17 km south of the financial hub of Makati. Comprising wide roads, clean air, little traffic and tight security, this upscale satellite town is developing a comfortable lifestyle of its own away from the central business district. On one corner lot stands a large modern house newly built for business couple Paul and Sharon Fernandez and their eight children. Before moving in, the young owners gave their architect, Manny Minana, *carte blanche* to express his contemporary design visions for their interiors as well.

The big family residence comprises a white modernist space as its basic canvas. There's a living area with sliding glass doors opening to an airy *lanai* with direct access to the tropical garden, as well as a dining room and various other spaces. It's clean-lined and open-plan, providing an uncluttered background for a discriminating selection of modern furniture and contemporary art. Minana mixes classic modern furnishings from Minotti, FurnItalia and Padua International with bold abstract paintings—the finest modern artworks in town—from Galleria Duemila and Finale Inc.

It's this combination that enlivens and uplifts the interiors. The superb artwork moves the spirit energy—the *chi*—around the house, while iconic furniture pieces from Manila and Milan define the modern white spaces. There are distinctive metal and stone sculptures in the living and dining rooms and bright modern paintings in a variety of spots. Precise arrangements configure a narrative: Minana's intuitive use of scale and proportion is akin to that of conjuring geomancy by a *feng shui* master.

Says the architect and designer: "I admire the eclectic design aesthetic of New York designers Sheldon-Mindel. They take a clean, white international canvas, then mix in the classic shapes: A boxy sofa, a retro armchair, a dark '60s coffee table ... individual items that are modern, classic and subdued, so then the artworks can dominate the space. Ideally the Fernandez place, too, achieves a clarity and sweeping modernity through the character of the interiors enlivened by art."

Previous pages A golden moon painting called *Bulan-bulan* by Leopoldo Aguilar Jr shines over the fine hardwood Jorn dining set by Minotti. Set off by a fuschia wall chosen by Mrs Fernandez, it is complemented by the Vertigo pendant lamp and Artemide standing lamp from Dexterton. A stainless bowl from FurnItalia sits central.

Left On the *lanai*, a giant paperclip sculpture by National Artist Arturo Luz is complemented inside by bold graphic artworks by Waling-Waling Gorospe and Tony Twigg—plus a pedestaled sculpture also by Luz.

Above Furniture art with modern art characterizes the spacious living room. The soft furniture in black, cream and chrome is from Minotti, while the Arco floor lamp with its elegant sweeping curves is from Steltz. The red Ovo-Celia chaises longues are from Padua International. Artworks, left to right: Untitled sculpture by Ramon Diaz; *Moving On #8* mural by Rock Drilon; *Seed* in black granite by Impy Pilapil.

Right More artwork on the dining side, left to right: *Design for Canopy* by Pardo de Leon; *Marble* by Impy Pilapil; and *Structures* by Tony Twigg.

Above Sunlight over the stairs passes through transparent railings. The extra wide hallway is marked by smart leather seats from Minotti.

Left View toward the upper gallery that leads to the bedrooms. Here, the designer conjures an exhibition at the top of the stairs, displaying large modern works from Finale Gallery.

Right The hallway of graphic impact: black console by Minotti is straddled by a pair of red seats by La Palma OC and balanced off by *Moving On #6* painting by Rock Drilon. In the background we see a photograph by Denise Weldon and and standing metal letter sculpture by Arturo Luz.

Below left and right The foyer vignette: A diptych abstract by Pardo de Leon welcomes one to the home; it's a tranquil expression when paired with a corded leather Ovo-Minay wing chair from Padua. Vignette in the *sala*: Padua's bright red Ovo-Celia lounger echoes the swirls of Drilon's mural painting. Note the bronze totem by Duddley Diaz.

Above left and right Hand-woven corded leather furniture pieces make artful accents: Low-backed Bernardo armchair on the left, and modernist Ovo-Lexus lounger on the right. Both from Padua International.

Below The rear elevation at dusk displays the clean linearity of the home. Overhangs from the roof and over the outdoor *lanai* provide shade and protection during the day.

Above The residence comprises a white modernist artwork built of space, light and fine art. Upstairs screens outside the oversized glass windows are echoed by the use of Venetian blinds downstairs—both provide protection from the tropical sun.

Previous pages The L-shaped bungalow comprises a tropical *lanai* in the main block; bedrooms and dining room in the extension; and a fern garden at their junction.

Above The family meets all day round a casual wood trestle table amid travertine walls, sandstone floors, and comfy rattan seating.

Left The rustic stone wall—a trickling installation in sound and temperature—was made (painstakingly) from finely chipped and hand-layered Mindoro stone.

Right Sturdy abaca weaves and contemporary colors outfit the family *lanai*, where guests gather round a male danseur sculpture by Jordan Mendoza.

This house of earthly delights was the creation of three artists—the architect Anna Sy, interior designer Yola Johnson, and ballerina-homemaker Sofia Zobel Elizalde—dancing between the members of her creative team. "I like to combine the sleek and modern with the colorful and comfortable, the classic and the modern, the antique and the updated," says Sofia on her contemporary abode.

Anna Sy planned the house to fit Sofia's taste for "a very open, tropical house…one with references to the Philippine context with a restful, relaxed attitude within." She chose a varied palette of materials: rustic green Mindoro stone for outer walls; semi-filled travertine for inner walls; and smooth Indonesian sandstone for floors. All three are fully visible at the heart of the house—the central, congenial *lanai*.

It is here that the Elizaldes spend most of their time, so after the laying of cool stones came the layering of warmth. Softening the *lanai*'s straight edges and bold lines was a priority. Yola Johnson achieved this with the addition of comfy sofas and rattan dining chairs; soft furnishings in shades of coral and white to match the owners' shell collections; the arrangement of traditional Philippine wood pieces; and the views of a leafy garden. She added chic modern colors and natural fibers, as well as a finely-crafted waterfall wall in Mindoro stone. The overall result is a gracious space, perfect for entertaining.

Elsewhere, Johnson continues the Made-in-Philippines' theme. The wine-colored dining room includes gauzy abaca curtains and decorative *capiz* shell chandeliers, while upstairs, a family room features dark *kamagong* furniture with plump cushions. Abaca drapes work well with the eggplant-colored walls and khaki-colored rug and sofa.

There's an interesting aside to the whole story of how the Elizades chose the plot: When the couple first started to look for a property, they discovered this odd, hexagonal-shaped lot that "felt somehow welcoming" and decided to take it. It was only later that they learned it had been the garden of the old Hagedorn family—where they themselves had played as children! Perhaps that's why they feel so at home when entertaining on their gracious *lanai* poised between a trickling waterfall and the wide green yard. "We love to entertain outdoors on our big *lanai* without aircon," says the dance mistress, "We listen to the sounds of water trickling over Mindoro stone and it feels like a constant homecoming."

Above The formal dining room with a burgundy wall features a giant mirror, gauzy abaca curtains, and twin chandeliers in black and white *capiz* shell.

Left Ensuring privacy, the guest suite occupies a separate unit in pavilion style near the main entrance. It has its own private cozy garden accessed through French doors.

Opposite top The inviting family lounge upstairs is characterized by comfort: low-level sofas, dark eggplant-colored walls and curtains, and an heirloom collection of antique maps of Asia.

Right Two Philippine *butaka* armchairs gaze toward the family pool by the peripheral wall—a rustic fence made of the same layered Mindoro stone as the waterfall.

ECLECTIC ASIAN

When re-modeling her old Makati home, jewelry designer Wynn Wynn Ong became an imaginative, design-driven force to be reckoned with. She worked on the project with good friend and architect Ed Calma in a creative collaboration that left both highly inspired. Ong loves bright colors, edgy art and bold accents and was able to express her personality in her new abode—with cultural references to Burma and the Philippines, her two Asian homes.

At first glance the highly exuberant style of Ong and the cooler, modernist ethos of an architect who designs with a Bauhaus eye might have seemed at odds. Yet, somehow, the two managed to produce something eclectic that works. The first job was to reconfigure the split-level house; the second was to expand the space; the third was to fill it.

At the entrance, a faux-stone gateway pivots open to reveal a sculpture terrace, then it is through the front door where one is confronted by a 19th century Vietnamese Gothic altar mysteriously floating on an aubergine wall. A few steps in, plentiful glazing and water features draw the eye, while furniture is arranged around Calma's signature white staircase. Hugging it is the central living room, a seamless gallery of clean white walls and sharp edges, providing a neutral backdrop for Ong's love of art and color.

The modernist home integrates Philippine-made furniture and contemporary Asian art with great flair. The *sala* showcases an array of contemporary sofas in pale Asian silk-linen and Philippine *kamagong* wood designed by Calma, while Ong designed the round coffee table from grey glass and salvaged beams. Two armchairs in skin, hardwood and crocodile leather make a further statement. Then there's the "edgy" artwork by young Asian artists, a collection of provocative images that keeps the home high-spirited. Giant canvases bearing bold figures by Maya Munoz, Jason Oliviera and Eric Chang mingle with organic sculptures by Juan Alcazaren, Dei Jardiniano and Inday Cadapan.

Upstairs, the creativity continues. The smokey-hued master bedroom features two women artists, Mia Herbosa and Debbie del Pan, "to keep me company on melancholy days". In Ong's view art has to be visceral; and her pieces resonate with her and her new home "with a touch of mystery".

Right This impressive array of six contemporary oil-on-parchment paintings by young artist Jason Oliviera were sourced at curator Jun Villalon's modernist Drawing Room.

Below The owner mixes antique *santos* (saint figures) with a hyper-real painting by Tatong Recheta Torres. Such pairings are not uncommon in the home, where new and old mingle with unusual results.

Previous pages The front door opens to reveal a 19th century Vietnamese Gothic altar hung on an accent wall, then a 90 degree angle turn reveals a spacious living room.

Right The living room is built around Calma's signature staircase. An open kitchen and dining room lie on the lower level, behind trim white shades (that are raised at all times).

Above A modern dining room is decorated with traditional artifacts where the warmth of wood shines through: Antiques from churches are integrated with contemporary Asian art with great aplomb. The nude torso in wood is by Gerry Araos.

Left A giant Burmese-looking portrait at the landing of the stairs is by Maya Munoz. The Ong home's creativity is seen in its collection of new Asian art.

Above The four-windowed master bedroom features the work of two women artists, Mia Herbosa (left) and Debbie del Pan (right), as well as a small lounging area on left.

Right The rebuilt home bears a modernist profile from the front entry steps up from the sidewalk. Ed Calma's micro-sliced real slate-veneered door pivots open to a raised deck—reserved for an old family tree and new sculptures.

COLLECTOR'S RETREAT

When popular television personality Kim Atienza inherited the compound of Joe Salazar in Malate, he promised the late designer that he would preserve his garden intact. "We've only redone the house interiors," explains the media advocate for modern art and live animals. "The garden is still Joe's. Besides, how can you improve on perfection?".

Certainly, the celebrated couturier's lush tropical garden is an impressive sight. There are giant *balete* trees, a brick tunnel gate, as well as a bridge over a *koi* pond. And now there's a remodeled house, re-worked to accommodate Atienza's young family, his mini zoo and his "obsessive" art collection. Somehow, knowing the garden is cared for by Atienza makes a kind of karmic sense.

In public, Atienza is known as an advocate for responsible pet care and animal conservation; in private, he manages a personal zoo of mini pinschers, tortoises, lizards, pythons and two hornbills who are his watch-birds. His elegant wife Felicia Hung, who recently founded the Chinese International School in Fort Bonifacio, is also an animal lover. Together they enjoy Salazar's woody-organic home, now spilling over with social realist artworks, modern wood sculptures and freeform organic chairs, many by Gerry Araos, sculptor of wood and fantasy landscapes. They are also justifiably proud of their collection of retro-modern classic chairs bought from old Chinatown shops and new-age dealers.

The couple entertains in a spacious *sala* built on polished hardwood floors—with the retro furniture marking the functions. At one end is a solid wood dining table surrounded by a variety of designer chairs of different ages and provenance. At the opposite end is a mixed-media setting of three retro classics under a swooping Arco lamp—with Araos' crocodile see-saws and Santiago Bose's seminal Fil-Am painting in attendance. From all angles, the "creatively cluttered" house is a gallery of cutting-edge art of the social commentary kind: modern artworks by Charlie Co, Elmer Borlongan, Geraldine Javier, Alfred Esquillo and Santi Bose (Atienza's irreverent close friend).

In one quiet corner of the couturier's former atelier there remains a life-sized terracotta portrait by sculptress Julie Lluch: This is Joe Salazar in clay, still present and enjoying his house and garden in old Malate.

Previous pages The Atienzas' *sala* spills over with social realist artworks with edgy stories to tell. On the walls: *Free Trade*, a Fil-Am commentary by Santiago Bose, and the disturbing *Ma McKinley* by Alfredo Esquillo. The *narra* wood floor holds torsos and rocking crocodiles by sculptor Gerry Araos.

Opposite top The dining area, marked with *molave* trunks in the corners, usually displays a dozen retro-classic chairs that Atienza sources from sundry shops. The architectural painting on the right is an Arturo Luz. The figure in the niche is the owner's mascot *santo* that survived a fire.

Left In the spare and modern kitchen, conversation begins round a stainless steel table with organic free-form chairs by sculptor Gerry Araos. The kitchen centerpiece is the *War-Dance* mural by social artist Charlie Co.

Opposite below left The back room displays Atienza's favorite paintings by Elmer Borlongan, Geraldine Javier and Charlie Co. Frames are propped round a life-sized bust sculpted by Julie Lluch—a clay portrait of couturier Joe Salazar.

Opposite below right Kim Atienza collects these quirky free-form saddles and back-seats in Philippine hardwoods; creative woodworks are by sculptor and landscaper Gerry Araos.

ACKNOWLEDGMENTS

Thanks to Gracious Homeowners

Ben Chan
Fritz and Sharon Azanza
Rikki and Beng Dee
Lor and Telly Calma
Norby and Wynn Wynn Ong
Kim and Felicia Atienza
Joey and Marissa Concepcion
Rico and Tina Ocampo
Ronnie and Laura Rodrigo
Joaquin and Prisilla Yap
Manolo and Norma Agoho
Charles and Ginette Dumancas
Felix Barrientos and Reggie Jacinto
Anton and Lisa Ongpin Periquet
Patxi and Sophia Zobel Elizalde
Danilo and Mellissa Gervacio
Paul and Sharon Fernandez
Mike and Marlene Pena
Ponce Veridiano
And other homeowners who declined to be named.

Hats-off to Architects and Designers:

Ed Ledesma
Ed Calma
Joey Yupangco
Gil Cosculuela
Miguel Pastor
Mike Pena
Lor Calma
Emmanuel Minana
Noel Saratan
Budji Layug & Royal Pineda
Ivy & Cynthia Almario
Ramon Antonio
Anton R Mendoza
Tina Periquet
Joy P Dominguez
Yola P Johnson
Kathleen Henares
Tes Pasola
J Anton Mendoza
Ana Rocha
Anna Sy
Jorge Yulo
And to Aida Concepcion Caluag for many styling favors.

Special *Salamat* to Furnishing Suppliers
For generous loans of fine furnishings.

(European Designs)
MegaMax Concepts (Marlene Ong)—Natuzzi, Vitra
MOS Design Bldg, Bonifacio High Street, Global City, Fort Taguig
+ 632 856-2748

ABITARE Internazionale Inc (Filaine Tan)—B&B ITALIA
GF Crown Tower, 107 HV dela Costa St, Salcedo Vill, Makati 1227
+632 892-1887

Living Innovations (Ferdinand Ong)—Minotti, Casamilano
2nd fl Makati Shangri-La Retail Arcade, Ayala Ave, Makati
+632 830-2230, 752-2768

FurnItalia (Florence Ko)—Molteni, Cassina
30th St cor Rizal Drive, Crescent Park, West Bonifacio,
Global City, Fort Taguig
+653 819-1887

(Philippine Furnishing Designs)
PADUA International (Vincent Padua)
1171-/A Mabini St, Ermita, Manila
+632 526-7772

OMO DESIGNS (Milo Naval)
Ste 129 LRI Design Plaza, 210 Nicanor Garcia St, Makati
+632 403-1209

A11 COLLECTION (Eric Paras)
2680 F B Harrison St, Pasay City 1300
+632 832-9972

B-AT-HOME (Budji Layug)
Nicanor Garcia St, Makati
+632 896-8348

OLD ASIA (Monette Mapa)
Power Plant Mall, Rockwell Center, Makati City 1200
+632 898-1314

***Grazie Tanto* to Artists and Galleries**
For loans of precious artworks and crafts.

Osmundo Esguerra (heirloom woodcraft)
Kenneth Cobonpue (organic-modernist furniture)
Tony Gonzales (shell and paper arts)
Tes Pasola (whimsical paper arts)
Louisa Robinson (shell and paper arts)
Maricris Brias (abaca fiber arts)
Ramon Orlina (glass art sculptures)
Impy Pilapil (metal and stone zen art)
Arturo Luz (National Artist sculptures)

Duemila Gallery (Silvana Diaz)
Finale Gallery (Vita Sarenas)
Hiraya Gallery (Didi Dee)
The Drawing Room (Jun Villalon)
Firma (Chito Vijandre & Ricky Toledo)
Demex Rattancraft, Inc (molded rattan jars)
EZRA Export Int'l (giant vine planters)
Dexterton (modern light fixtures)